WICKED BUGS

also by AMY STEWART

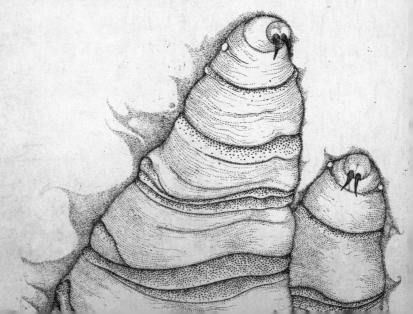

Wicked Bugs

THE LOUSE THAT CONQUERED
NAPOLEON'S ARMY & OTHER
DIABOLICAL INSECTS

Amy Stewart

ⴴ ETCHINGS AND DRAWINGS BY ⴴ

Briony Morrow-Cribbs

Algonquin Books of Chapel Hill

2011

Published by
ALGONQUIN BOOKS OF CHAPEL HILL
Post Office Box 2225
Chapel Hill, North Carolina 27515-2225

a division of
WORKMAN PUBLISHING
225 Varick Street
New York, New York 10014

Reproduction of the Schmidt Pain Index (pages 137–138) reprinted by permission of Justin O. Schmidt.

Library of Congress Cataloging-in-Publication Data
Stewart, Amy.
Wicked bugs : the louse that conquered Napoleon's army & other
diabolical insects / Amy Stewart ; etchings and drawings by
Briony Morrow-Cribbs.—1st ed
    p. cm.
Includes bibliographical references and index.
ISBN 978-1-56512-960-3
1. Insect pests.   2. Arachnida.   I. Morrow-Cribbs, Briony.   II. Title.
SB931.S83 2011
632'.7—dc22   2011003629

10 9 8 7 6 5 4 3 2 1
First Edition

To PSB

CONTENTS

CONTENTS

END NOTES

WARNING:
We Are Seriously
Outnumbered

I n 1909, the *Chicago Daily Tribune* ran an article titled "If Bugs Were the Size of Men." It began with this ominous statement: "All the powers of destruction that were ever invented by man are puerile and absurd compared with those with which nature has invested insects." The reporter went on to ask what would happen "if some mighty magician's wand should be waved over the world tomorrow and mankind be reduced to the size of insects, while these tiny creatures should reach the size of men."

Chicagoans must have read with alarm of the calamities that would befall them if they were to trade places with bugs: the giant Hercules beetle was not just formidable, but immoral, with a taste for drinking and brawling; bark beetles would mow down massive fortresses; armies would be helpless against the artillery of the bombardier beetle; and spiders would "destroy elephants . . . a man's only possible salvation would be that he was too insignificant to attack." Even lions would cower in fear against these new winged and multilegged enemies.

The reporter's intent was, undoubtedly, to make the point that insects are powerful in their own way and to suggest that only their diminutive size keeps them from conquering the world.

If only that were true. In fact, insects have changed the course of history. They have halted soldiers in their tracks. They have driven farmers off their land. They have devoured cities and forests, and inflicted pain, suffering, and death upon hundreds of millions.

This is not to say that they don't do good as well. They pollinate the plants that feed us, and they are themselves food for creatures up and down the food chain. They do the vital work of decomposition, returning everything from fallen leaves to fallen heroes back to the earth. Any number of insects, from the blow fly to the blister beetle, have proven useful in medicine. And they prey on one another, keeping pests in check. We could not live without them. In fact, indiscriminate pesticide use and destruction of insect habitats is far more harmful than simply learning to live alongside them and to appreciate their finer qualities.

But this is not a book celebrating their virtues. As with *Wicked Plants,* I have devoted myself exclusively to the dark side of the relationship between nature and humans. Some might say that people already harbor enough hatred of insects and need no further encouragement. And those of us who are staunchly on the side of bugs, sweeping them gently out of the house with a word of kindness and refusing to allow chemical sprays into our gardens for fear of disturbing their dinner, might be disinclined to explore their criminal history.

However, our affections can be as misleading as our phobias. The common garden spider on your windowsill deserves applause for her good deeds, but the bloodsucking assassin bug you encounter on a South American vacation should be given a wide berth. Learning to make such distinctions doesn't require an entomology degree; a little common sense and an open-minded curiosity is all you need. I hope that *Wicked Bugs* inspires both — and delivers a few spine-tingling thrills along the way.

I am not a scientist or doctor. I'm a writer who is fascinated by the natural world. Within each chapter, I set out to tell a deliciously frightening story and to offer just enough information about the habits and lifestyles of each creature to make them easier to recognize. This is by no means a comprehensive field guide or a medical reference book; please do not rely upon it to definitively identify a bug or diagnose an ailment. For that, there is a list of recommended reading and resources at the end of the book.

Of the thousands of species I could have included, I chose those that intrigued me the most. I use the word *wicked* rather broadly, encompassing the world's most painful insects, such as the bullet ant, which gets its name from the fact that its bite feels like a gunshot wound; its most destructive insects, like the Formosan subterranean termite quietly chewing away at the seams of the floodwalls around New Orleans; and disease vectors like the Oriental rat flea that brought the Black Death to Europe. Insects that destroy crops, drive people from their homes, or simply drive people mad all found a place within these pages. Some of the stories are grotesque, and some are tragic, but in every case, I was left awestruck by the power and intricacy of these tiny creatures.

Entomologists will be quick to protest that the term *bug* is misleading, and they are quite right. Most of us use the word to describe any number of tiny slithering and crawling creatures; we deploy it with even less precision when we use it to refer to an illness like the stomach flu, a flaw in a computer program, or a listening device hidden in a lampshade. None of these are, from a scientific perspective, accurate. Strictly speaking, an insect is a creature with six legs, a three-segmented body, and usually two sets of wings. A true bug is a subset of insect in the order Hemiptera that has piercing and sucking mouthparts. An aphid, therefore, is a type of insect that we can properly call a bug; an ant is not. Spiders, worms, centipedes, slugs, and scorpions are not insects at all but arachnids and other classes of creatures that are only distantly related to insects. I could not resist including a few of them in this book and beg the forgiveness of scientists for employing the amateur's definition of the term *bug* to refer to them all.

To date, over one million species of insects have been described worldwide. It is estimated that there are ten quintillion insects alive on the planet right now, which means that for each one of us, there are two hundred million of them. If you arranged all living creatures on earth into a pyramid, almost all of it would be made up of insects, spiders, and the like. Other animals—including people—would form only the smallest section in one corner of the pyramid. We are seriously outnumbered.

To insects and their squirming, wriggling, and crawling compatriots, I offer my wary respect and unabashed awe. After all I've learned, I still can't bring myself to squash a bug. But I watch them now with more amazement—and alarm—than ever.

WICKED BUGS

African Bat Bug

AFROCIMEX CONSTRICTUS

When a North Carolina family discovered tiny, bloodsucking parasites resembling bed bugs in their home, they had no idea that there was worse news still to come. The bugs were a sign that bats had taken up residence in the attic.

Bat bugs are parasites that favor bats but seek out other warm-blooded creatures when they get exceedingly hungry. They don't need to eat often—an adult bat bug can survive on one blood meal per year—but in order to have the energy to reproduce, they dine repeatedly on the blood of live bats. The bugs don't live on the bats themselves; they hide in the warm, dry crevices of an attic or a hollow tree where bats also dwell, and they eat when the bats come home to roost in the early morning hours.

Alarmed by the presence of these bugs and the bats they feed upon, the family contacted an exterminator, who advised them to wait until fall, when the young bats would be old enough to fly out of the attic on their own. Then the cracks and crevices around the roof could be patched while the bats were away. Using this method, they even-

SIZE:
5 mm

FAMILY:
Cimicidae

HABITAT:
Close proximity to bat colonies, usually trees or caves, sometimes the eaves and attics of houses

DISTRIBUTION:
The African bat bug is native to East Africa, but other species of bat bugs are found worldwide wherever there are large populations of bats, including the American Midwest

tually succeeded in ridding their home of bats. Unfortunately, the bat bugs were not so easily evicted.

Once their hosts have left, bat bugs will wander the house and feed on humans. Signs of an infestation include flesh-colored welts on the skin, often in groups of two or three, and itching. The bites are generally harmless, although they could become inflamed or infected from too much scratching. The bugs themselves are rarely spotted as they typically feed while the host is sleeping. At only one-eighth of an inch long, oval-shaped, and dark red in color, they are almost indistinguishable from their close relative, the bed bug.

In laboratories, colonies of bat bugs quickly go extinct because the females simply cannot escape the painful and destructive attentions of the males.

While it may be uncomfortable for humans to share a house with these creatures, it's nothing compared to what female bat bugs experience when they engage in that most intimate of acts with a member of the opposite sex. All species of bat bugs participate in a form of lovemaking called traumatic insemination, in which the male bypasses the female's vagina altogether and pierces her abdomen with his horribly sharp little penis. The sperm goes straight into the bloodstream, where some of it makes its way to her reproductive organs and the rest is simply absorbed and eliminated.

This is not at all an agreeable arrangement for female bat bugs. In laboratories, colonies of bat bugs quickly go extinct because the females simply cannot escape the painful and destructive attentions of the males long enough to heal and safely give birth. To get around this problem, the female of one subspecies, the African *Afrocimex constrictus,* developed an entirely new receptacle called a spermalege that is designed to redirect the male's repeated stabbings to one particular location in the abdomen where they can be more easily accommodated.

To further complicate matters, amorous males will also pierce the bodies of male bat bugs. The males, being even more displeased by this behavior than the females, have developed tougher versions of the spermalege in the hopes of protecting themselves against their sex-crazed brethren. This has worked so well that females have taken notice. They are beginning to copy the males, imitating the sturdier version of this false genitalia that the females invented in the first place. This extraordinary case of females-imitating-males-imitating-females has resulted in what one befuddled scientist called "a hotbed of deception" in the twisted world of bat bug romance.

Meet the Relatives The bat bug is closely related to bed bugs and a few other insects that make their living through hematophagy, the practice of feeding on the blood of warm-blooded animals.

SHE'S JUST NOT THAT INTO YOU

African bat bugs aren't the only creatures that suffer for love. Aggressive and adversarial mating practices are surprisingly common, making for some truly terrible dates. Here are just a few horror stories from the war between the sexes.

BANANA SLUG *Ariolimax californicus*

These slugs are an astonishing sight on the forest floor: they are longer than a finger and bright yellow, the precise color of a banana. They're found all along the West Coast, particularly in California, where they are prized as a kind of strange local treasure. The University of California at Santa Cruz has even adopted the slug as its school mascot.

For such seemingly peaceable creatures, they engage in very violent sex. Banana slugs are hermaphrodites—possessing both male and female sexual organs—and when they are ready to mate, they leave a trail of slime that acts as a signal to potential partners. As a kind of foreplay, two slugs will eat each other's slime. Then they size each other up—literally. Because the slugs penetrate each other simultaneously, they try to find partners of roughly the same length to avoid getting stuck. As they get closer to each other, wrapping into an S shape to facilitate mating, they often bite one another. This is normal premating behavior for a slug, but it leaves them both gouged and battered.

The slugs may remain intertwined for several hours. When they finally begin to disengage, it is not uncommon for them to find that they've become hopelessly stuck to one another, leaving a slug with no choice but to chew off its partner's penis. This behavior, known as apophallation, might seem like an evolutionary dead end. But in fact, the slug survives and can go on to mate again, playing only the part of the female.

FIREFLY *Photuris versicolor*

Fireflies use their charming display of lights to signal to one another during summer courtship rituals. The males fly around at night, flashing their lights and hoping to attract a female. Each species communicates with its own distinct pattern of long and short flashes so that it won't attract a female of the wrong species. The females respond with a flash of light of their own, and their reply is species-specific, too: the length of time that passes between the male's signal and the female's response is different for every species, and it is this small difference in signals that allows compatible fireflies to find one another.

That system works fairly well until a *femme fatale* firefly belonging to the species *Photuris versicolor* gets involved. She sends out one pattern of light to attract a mate, but also emits a deceptive signal to attract the male of another species, *Photinus ignites*. If she can convince him to come near her, she attacks and eats him. But the male of this species is more than just dinner for her—in eating him, she takes on some of the defensive chemicals that he uses to keep predators away. Those chemicals protect not just her, but her young as well.

PRAYING MANTID
Tenodera aridifolia sinensis

A female praying mantid doesn't always eat her mate, but it happens often enough to make male mantids nervous. Males approach with caution, first assessing whether the female has had anything to eat lately. If she looks well fed, the male has some hope of getting through the ordeal alive. If she's hungry, he might look for another partner or jump on her from a greater distance to avoid getting grabbed.

Despite the male's best efforts, females do tend to turn around and bite their partner's heads off during copulation. When this happens, he continues to mate with her, completing the act just as she finishes her dinner. By the end of their date there is nothing left of him but his wings.

The lucky male mantid that survives an encounter with a female is often seen perched on top of her for a few moments afterward. This is not a sign of affection; it's something more like fear. Males who have made it this far know better than to make any sudden movements. They dismount slowly, with great caution, in hopes of making a safe and quiet escape.

Males approach with caution, first assessing whether the female has had anything to eat lately. If she looks well fed, the male has some hope of getting through the ordeal alive.

GOLDEN ORB-WEAVER *Nephila plumipes*

This Australian spider is remarkably cannibalistic. Roughly 60 percent of sexual encounters end with the female eating the male, and, in fact, the males make up a significant part of the females' nutritional intake. To make matters worse, the males are often unable to disentangle themselves from their female partners without breaking off part of their own sexual organ and leaving it inside the female.

While this could be seen as a genetic advantage—in the bug world it is not uncommon for males to leave behind a "genital plug" that prevents other males from mating with their chosen partner—this does not appear to be the case with *Nephila plumipes*. Other males are perfectly capable of mating with a female, simply working around the wreckage of her last encounter.

Researchers have said that because of this injury, "males can expect a limited mating success even if they survive copulation . . . Thus, the costs of post-mating cannibalism for males may be rather small." In other words, with no prospects of another sexual encounter in their future, they might as well get eaten—at least providing one decent meal for the mother of their children as their final act of parenthood.

CRAB SPIDER *Xysticus cristatus*, others

Considering the hazards of lovemaking faced by males in the arachnid and insect worlds, it is no wonder that some species of crab spiders have come up with another plan. Male crab spiders have been observed approaching females cautiously, tapping on them to gauge their readiness for courtship, and then quickly wrapping a few silky threads around the female's legs to hold her down during mating. This form of bondage is politely referred to as a bridal veil by scientists who have observed the ritual.

Asian Giant Hornet

VESPA MANDARINIA JAPONICA

I n the last few years, during dry summers, public health officials in Tokyo have warned citizens that the world's largest and most painful hornet may be in their midst. The so-called Asian giant hornet, known locally as yak-killer, delivers a venomous sting that contains high levels of the pain-inducing compounds normally found in bee or wasp stings, along with a deadly neurotoxin called mandaratoxin that can be fatal. The world's leading expert in the giant hornet, Masato Ono, described the sting as feeling like "a hot nail through my leg." Worst of all, the sting attracts other hornets to the victim through the pheromones it leaves behind, increasing the likelihood of being stung several times.

SIZE:
50 mm

FAMILY:
Vespidae

HABITAT:
Forests and, increasingly, cities

DISTRIBUTION:
Japan, China, Taiwan, Korea, and other areas throughout Asia

In Japan these hornets are called *suzumebachi,* which translates to "sparrow wasp." They are so large, measuring five centimeters from head to tail, that when they fly they actually resemble small birds. During hot summers they can be seen in Japanese cities foraging in garbage cans for bits of discarded fish to carry back to their young. Because they are so willing to venture into urban areas in search of food, about forty people die every year after being stung by the massive hornets.

If such a creature is frightening to humans, imagine what it must look like to a honeybee. Scientists observing wild colonies of the Japanese honeybee, *Apis cerana japonica,* have long known that the colonies are vulnerable to attacks from the giant hornets. Usually a single hornet shows up first to scout the area. It kills a few bees and brings them back to the hive to feed its young. After more of these trips, the hornet tags the hive by smearing it with pheromones, signaling that it is time for an attack.

A gang of about thirty hornets descend on the hive, and within a few hours these monstrous creatures massacre as many as thirty thousand of the small honeybees, ripping off their heads and tossing their bodies on the ground. Once they've killed the bees, the hornets occupy the empty hive for about ten days, robbing it of its honey and stealing the bee larvae to feed their own children.

Recently, Masato Ono and his colleagues at Tamagawa University discovered that the Japanese honeybees had devised an extraordinarily clever way of attacking back. The first time a solitary hornet approaches the hive, worker bees retreat inside, luring the hornet to the entrance. Then an army of over five hundred honeybees surround the hornet, beating their wings furiously and raising the surrounding temperature to 116 degrees—just hot enough to kill the hornet.

This is a dangerous procedure for the honeybees: if the swarm gets just a few degrees hotter, it will kill them as well. In fact, some worker bees do die in the struggle, but the swarm pushes them out of the way and carries on until the hornet is dead. It can take twenty minutes for the honeybees to bake their enemy to death. While it is not unusual for insects to mount a group defense against an enemy, this is the only known case of using body heat alone to defeat an attacker.

The world's leading expert in the giant hornet described the sting as feeling like "a hot nail through my leg."

The hornets' extraordinary strength led Japanese researchers to test an extract of their stomach juices as a performance enhancement for athletes. They discovered that adult hornets, which can fly incredible distances in search of food, are actually unable to eat much solid food themselves because their digestive tracts are so small. However, they do bring dead insects back to their young to eat. After the larvae have finished their meal, the adults tap on their heads, which prompts the larvae to offer up a "kiss" consisting of a few drops of clear liquid. The adults drink this liquid, using it as a source of fuel. The Japanese scientists harvested the clear liquid, one drop at a time, from larvae they found in over eighty hornets' nests. In the laboratory they demonstrated that both mice and graduate students showed reduced fatigue and an increased ability to turn fat into energy after drinking the juice.

Marathon runner Naoko Takahashi, who won an Olympic gold medal in Sydney in 2000, credited her success to this "hornet juice." As a natural substance, it didn't violate the International Olympic Committee rules on performance enhancers. Today an athletic drink called hornet juice is marketed to athletes with the claim that it boosts endurance. However, these drinks don't contain actual extracts from giant hornet larvae, just a mix of amino acids intended to mimic the powerful juice.

Meet the Relatives Giant Asian hornets are related to other hornets, which are distinguished from wasps by their larger heads and more rounded abdomens. The European hornet, *Vespa crabro*, delivers a nasty sting when disturbed, but it is no more deadly than the sting of any other hornet.

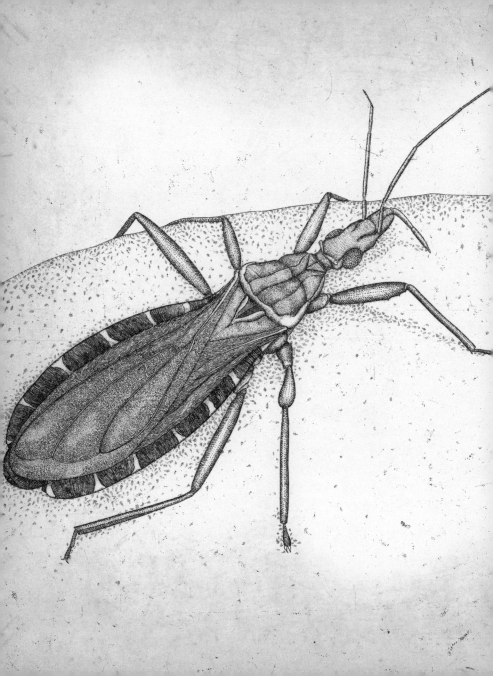

Assassin Bug

TRIATOMA INFESTANS

In 1835, a young Charles Darwin recorded a strange encounter with a bug in Argentina. He was near the end of his journey on board the HMS *Beagle,* a British naval ship charged with surveying South America. Darwin had been hired on to fulfill the roles of scholarly companion to the captain and ship's naturalist. The journey had already been fraught with peril: the captain was unstable and ill-tempered; the locals attacked the crew and robbed them; and most everyone was beset by illness or hunger at some point. Then, on March 25, Darwin himself became dinner for one of the region's bloodsucking insects. In his diary he wrote, "At night I experienced an attack (for it deserves no less a name) of the Benchuca, a species of Reduvius, the great black bug of the Pampas. It is most disgusting to feel soft wingless insects, about an inch long, crawling over one's body."

He also recounted an experiment in which several of his shipmates offered themselves up to the bloodthirsty beasts: "When placed on a table, and though surrounded by people, if a finger was

SIZE:
15–25 mm

FAMILY:
Reduviidae

HABITAT:
Generally found near prey, which could mean homes, barns, nests, caves, or any shelters where birds, rodents, or other animals live

DISTRIBUTION:
North and South America; some species in India and Southeast Asia

presented, the bold insect would immediately protrude its sucker, make a charge, and if allowed, draw blood . . . This one feast, for which the benchuca was indebted to one of the officers, kept it fat during four whole months; but, after the first fortnight, it was quite ready to have another suck."

What Darwin didn't know—what no one knew at the time—was that the bite of some assassin bugs can transmit a fatal illness called Chagas disease. These large, oval-shaped insects belong to the family Reduviidae; within that family, there are about 138 species of the bloodsucking *Triatoma* genus worldwide, half of which are known to transmit the disease. Most are found in North and South America, although there are some species in India and Southeast Asia. They live quite comfortably alongside their hosts, hiding out in burrows and nests and feeding on small rodents or bats. They're not shy about moving into houses or barns, either. In some parts of Latin America, where palm fronds are used as roofing material, the bugs are inadvertently introduced to local households through eggs attached to the fronds.

Assassin bugs go through five nymph stages on their way to adulthood, drinking up to nine times their weight in blood during a single feeding. An adult female might live six months, and during that time, she'll lay one hundred to six hundred eggs, the precise number depending on how much blood she consumes.

In most cases, the bite of the assassin bug causes no pain. It may feed for just a few minutes or up to half an hour, its body growing engorged as it drinks. A home with a severe infestation might contain several hundred bugs, and in this case it would not be uncommon for as many as twenty bugs to feed on an individual person, taking one to three milliliters of blood per night. Health care workers visiting the homes of patients recognize the worst infestations of these bugs by the streaks of black-and-white waste products running down the walls.

The assassin bug's preference for feeding around the mouth of its victim has earned it the nickname "kissing bug"; unfortunately, it can be the kiss of death. In 1908 a Brazilian doctor named Carlos Chagas was studying malaria when he noticed this bloodsucking insect and decided to find out whether it was carrying any disease-causing microbes. What he found was a protozoan parasite called *Trypanosoma cruzi* that the bug takes in during a meal. The parasite develops and multiplies inside the gut of the bug, and is then excreted in its feces. People get infected by the disease not from the bite itself, but from the feces deposited on the skin of the victim while the bug feeds. Scratching or rubbing the bug bite pushes the waste into the wound, introducing it to the bloodstream. (North American assassin bugs wait to do their business until about a half hour after they have eaten, by which time they have moved away from the victim. This helps explain why the disease is less common in the United States.)

What is most remarkable about Chagas's discovery is that he found the disease inside the vector insect first, then went on to diagnose humans who were infected with it. Once he did, he realized that he'd stumbled across a fatal disease that seemed to be linked to colonization. As settlers cleared land in the jungle and built mud and palm-thatched huts, the assassin bugs that were already living in the jungle and carrying the disease from one rodent to another found themselves suddenly living among humans—a fantastic source of warm, rich blood. Although the locals had already named the bug—some called it *vinchuca,* which meant "that which lets itself fall" from the roof, and some called it *chirimacha,* which meant "that which fears the cold"—the disease caused by the bug was just starting to become widespread around the time Chagas discovered it.

The assassin bug's preference
for feeding around the mouth
of its victim has earned it
the nickname "kissing bug";
unfortunately, it can be
the kiss of death.

People who are bitten around the eyes develop a terrible swelling. Bites elsewhere on the body result in small sores that give way to fever and swollen lymph nodes. The disease can kill in its early stages, but most people go on to experience a symptomless phase, followed by extensive damage to the heart, intestines, and other major organs, which may ultimately be fatal. About three hundred thousand people in the United States live with Chagas disease, and eight to eleven million people throughout Latin America suffer from it. Although early treatment can kill the parasites, there is no treatment for the later stages.

Some historians speculate that Charles Darwin himself was infected with Chagas disease and ultimately died from it. This would explain some of the strange and complicated health problems that plagued him throughout his life. However, the fact that he seems to have suffered from some of the same symptoms before he encountered the assassin bug in Argentina argues against that theory. Requests to exhume his remains from Westminster Abbey and test them for Chagas disease have been denied, leaving the exact cause of his health problems a mystery.

Meet the Relatives Wheel bugs, which prey upon caterpillars and other garden pests, are a type of assassin bug. Other relatives include the so-called thread-legged bugs, a group of long, skinny insects whose victims include spiders and other bugs.

BUGS OF WAR

Fifty years ago, in response to the launch of the Soviet satellite *Sputnik,* the U.S. Department of Defense formed a forward-thinking research office called DARPA, the Defense Advanced Research Projects Agency. Since then, DARPA researchers have developed stealth aircraft, new submarine technology, and an early version of the Internet, among other things. And now they've turned their attention to cyborg insects.

The Hybrid Insect Micro-Electro-Mechanical System (HI-MEMS) seeks to implant computer chips inside caterpillars before they undergo metamorphosis into moths or butterflies. Scientists hope to use that circuitry to remotely control the flight path of insects so that they can someday be used to fly into enemy locations and transmit intelligence without ever being detected.

While the HI-MEMS program sounds too strange and futuristic to be true, it is simply the latest in a long history of deploying insects in war. Entomologist Jeffrey Lockwood studies the use of bugs in warfare; his research reveals that even beloved insects like honeybees have been used with malicious intent.

BEES AND WASPS

Bees and wasps have been used as weapons for thousands of years. Hurling a beehive or wasp nest at an enemy is an effective way to create havoc and send even the fiercest warriors running. Mayans had been using them since 2600 BC; their legends describe the use of human dummies with a gourd filled with stinging insects for a head. Early Greek writings on warfare described the practice of building tunnels under enemy walls and releasing bees and wasps into the tunnels. The use of catapults to hurl hives over enemy walls dates back at least to Roman times and continued through the Middle Ages.

But bees weren't used only during ancient times. As recently as World War I, Tanzanians hid beehives in the undergrowth and rigged their lids with trip wires so that invading British troops would encounter them in their efforts to seize control of the area from the Germans.

One of the most intriguing uses of bees in warfare was recorded by a contemporary of Socrates named Xenophon. He described the use of poisoned hives in Greek warfare around 402 BC: "All the soldiers ate of the combs, lost their senses, vomited, and were affected with purging, and none of them were able to stand upright; such as had eaten a little were like men greatly intoxicated, and such as had eaten much were like mad-men, and some like persons at the point of death." The soldiers had, apparently, been given beehives filled with the honey of bees that had feasted on rhododendron and azalea, plants that produce neurotoxins so potent that they remain active in the honey. Those who eat the honey succumb to honey intoxication, also called grayanotoxin poisoning.

ASSASSIN BUGS

These bloodsucking creatures that transmit Chagas disease have been used as instruments of torture in so-called bug pits. The most well-known example comes from 1838, when a British diplomat named Charles Stoddart arrived in the city of Bukhara in Uzbekistan to try to win over the local emir and enlist his support in halting the expansion of the Russian empire. Instead of making friends, he was branded an enemy and thrown into the bug pit, a hole beneath the *zindan,* a traditional Central Asian prison. There he suffered the attacks of assassin bugs, which were kept alive in between prisoners with gifts of fresh meat. A stone chute delivered manure from the stables above, which further attracted bugs and generally made the pit a place of misery.

A fellow British officer, Arthur Conolly, tried to rescue Stoddart after a couple of years, but he, too, was thrown into the pit. The men were literally eaten alive; accounts of the few times they were seen aboveground describe them as covered in sores and lice. The insects did not kill them, however: to accomplish that, they were beheaded in a public ceremony in 1842.

SCORPIONS

Even when they don't sting, scorpions look terrifying. Pliny the Elder wrote in about 77 AD that the scorpion was "a dangerous scourge, and has venom like that of the serpent; with the exception that its effects are far more painful, as the person who is stung will linger for three days before death ensues." He added that the sting of a scorpion was "invariably fatal to virgins, and nearly always so to matrons."

In the ancient city of Hatra, not far from Kirkuk and Mosul in Iraq, scorpions were deployed by local leaders in about 198 AD. They were defending their walled city against an attack by Roman troops led by Septimius Severus. When the troops arrived, the leaders had filled clay pots with scorpions—probably collected from the surrounding desert—and readied these venomous bombs to hurl at their attackers. Herodian of Antioch, a Roman historian writing at the time, described the scene this way: "Making clay pots, they filled them with winged insects, little poisonous flying creatures. When these were hurled down on the besiegers, the insects fell into the Romans' eyes and on all the unprotected parts of their bodies; digging in before they were noticed, they bit and stung the soldiers." Although scorpions don't fly, historians believe that the bombs contained scorpions along with an assortment of stinging insects, perhaps also including bees and wasps.

FLEAS

These tiny, bloodsucking carriers of bubonic plague have also been used as an agent of war. During World War II, Japan's biological warfare project, called Unit 731, developed a method for dropping bombs filled with plague-infected fleas into enemy territory. They tested it in Ningbo, a seaside town in eastern China, and Changde, a city on the Yuan River in Hunan Province. Both communities experienced outbreaks of plague as a result of those experiments.

An estimated two hundred thousand Chinese people died at the hands of Japan's biological agent program. An operation called "Cherry Blossoms at Night" would have released the fleas over California, but that plan was never executed. The Japanese military also conducted horrific medical experiments on prisoners, subjecting them to gas chambers, disease, frostbite, and surgery without anesthetic. Although evidence of these war crimes did come to light after the war ended, the United States granted immunity to doctors involved with the project in exchange for access to their research and data. As part of the agreement, the project was kept a secret. It was not until the mid-1990s that historians began to report upon the atrocities committed by Unit 731.

He was branded an enemy and
thrown into the bug pit.
There he suffered the attacks of
assassin bugs, who were kept alive
in between prisoners with
gifts of fresh meat.

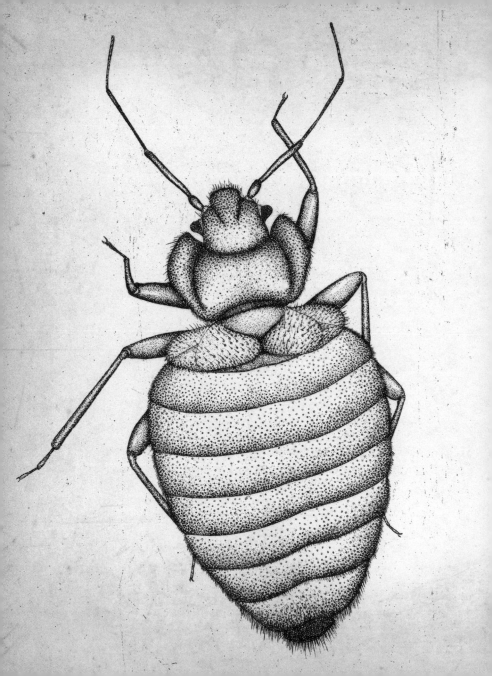

Bed Bug

CIMEX LECTULARIUS

In Toronto, a sixty-year-old man went to his doctor complaining of fatigue. He was diabetic, a recovering alcoholic with only a year's sobriety, and a former crack cocaine user, so fatigue was the least of his problems. But the doctor found severe anemia, which he treated with a prescription dose of iron. A month later the man was back with even worse symptoms, requiring a blood transfusion before he could return home. A few weeks later, he needed another transfusion. The blood loss was inexplicable and frightening.

SIZE:
4–5 mm

FAMILY:
Cimicidae

HABITAT:
Nests, caves, and other warm, dry places near food sources

DISTRIBUTION:
Temperate regions throughout the world

Then the doctor paid a call to his patient at home. The problem was immediately apparent: bed bugs were everywhere. He could even see them crawling on the man during the visit. The public health department was called in; after the apartment was sprayed with insecticide and the old furniture removed, the man gradually recovered.

The bed bug travels at night, lurking in low light, feeling its way toward warmth and the tantalizing odor of carbon dioxide. It approaches its dinner—that is, you—with outstretched antennae, gripping the skin tightly with tiny claws. Once it has a good grip, it begins rocking back and forth, working needlelike feeding organs called stylets into the skin. It bites gently, piercing the skin just enough to get the blood flowing. The stylets probe around under the skin in search of a good-sized blood vessel to tap into. The bed bug's saliva contains an anticoagulant to prevent clotting, so it can settle down and feed. If it is left alone to enjoy its meal, it will feed for about five minutes and then wander off. But if you were to swat at the bug in your sleep, it would probably move a short distance away and bite again, leading to a telltale series of three sequential puncture wounds. Dermatologists call these bites "breakfast, lunch, and dinner."

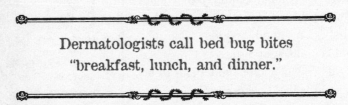

Dermatologists call bed bug bites "breakfast, lunch, and dinner."

Before World War II, bed bugs were a fact of life in the United States and around the world. Pesticides developed around that time helped eliminate them, but now the blood-sucking parasite is back. Reasons for its reappearance include an increase in international travel, a reduction in the use of broad-spectrum pesticides in favor of targeted baits, and, alarmingly, the bed bugs' own resistance to chemical controls. Researchers at the University of Massachusetts have reported that bed bugs in New York City show new mutations in nerve cells that allow them to survive exposure to neurotoxic ingredients in bug sprays. In particular, they found that pyrethroid sprays, the synthetic version of a natural insecticide derived from chrysanthemum flowers, had little effect on New York bed bugs, while a population collected in Florida was easily wiped out by the poisons.

What has this meant for the average New Yorker? Although bed bugs have not been shown to transmit disease, the bites can cause allergic reactions, swelling, rashes, and secondary infections from scratching. The blood loss from an infestation can be severe enough to cause anemia, particularly in children and people in poor health. The sleep loss and emotional distress alone are enough to bring on serious psychological problems.

A bed bug can survive up to a year without feeding. In the wild it might live in a nest or cave alongside its prey; in the city it prefers upholstery, loose wallpaper, or the dry, dark spaces behind pictures or inside light sockets. The worst outbreaks may be accompanied by streaks of feces along the tufts of upholstery. A strange sweet odor that comes from the bug's scent glands pervades homes with large populations of the bugs. The compounds it produces, hexanol and octenol, are used to communicate with other bed bugs, but the smell is a giveaway that trained dogs can detect even when people can't. It's been described as smelling like coriander—and in fact the name coriander comes from the word *koris*, which is Greek for bug. For the most part, the bugs don't travel around with people, although homeless people who don't change clothes often may find that bed bugs follow them everywhere, laying eggs inside clothing or even under overgrown toenails.

Controlling bed bugs is not easy, especially in apartment buildings, where they can move from one room to another via ductwork or cracks in the plaster. City dwellers are starting to avoid purchasing used furniture for fear of unwanted hitchhikers, and mattress companies have learned the hard way that using the same truck to haul away old mattresses and deliver new ones can perpetuate the very infestations that people are trying to eliminate.

One promising new control is an old-fashioned desiccant dust, messy but nontoxic, mixed with the bugs' own pheromones. This so-called alarm pheromone entices them to get up and move around, exposing them to enough of the desiccant to cause them to simply dry up and die. An even more natural form of pest control may show up all by itself: the house centipede, *Scutigera coleoptrata,* feeds on bed bugs, as does the so-called masked hunter, *Reduvius personatus,* an assassin bug that gets its blood meal by robbing bed bugs of theirs.

Meet the Relatives   The Cimicidae family includes not only bed bugs, but bat bugs and bird bugs as well; all depend on the blood of their prey for survival.

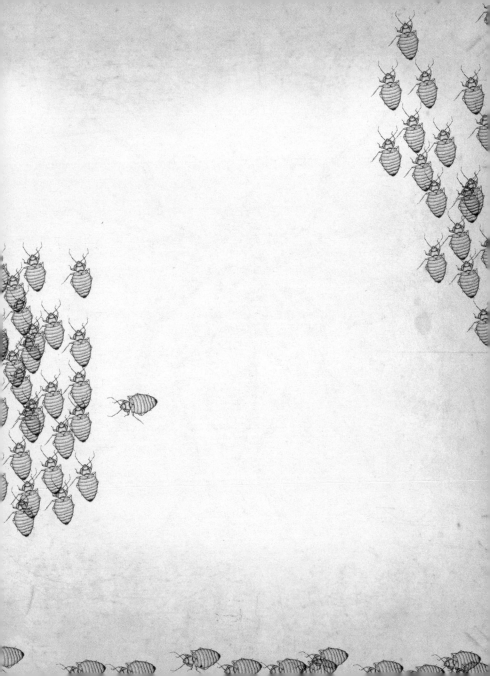

Biting Midge

CULICOIDES SPP.

"One midge is an entomological curiosity, a thousand can be hell!" So said Queensland scientist D. S. Kettle. He should know: the biting midge is such a serious pest in that part of Australia that it actually depresses property values. A 2006 study estimated that this tiny, bloodsucking annoyance was responsible for driving down real-estate prices to the tune of $25 to $50 million in the desirable Hervey Bay area, where new homes built close to mangrove swamps were plagued by the insects.

The midges posed such a problem that angry homeowners marched on city hall, demanding a solution, and there were even threats of violence against local officials. Soon a Biting Midge Investigative Committee was formed to combat the menace. According to a community report, "the strain of living with biting midge even caused marriages to break up," presumably because couples were forced to spend more time indoors together rather than enjoying the respite of an afternoon on the golf course. The community developed a program of insecticide spraying that was effective against

SIZE:
1–3 mm

FAMILY:
Ceratopogonidae

HABITAT:
Near beaches, lakes, bogs, and other damp areas; most active in humid, warm regions

DISTRIBUTION:
Primarily North and South America, Australia, and Europe, but also elsewhere throughout the world.

the midges and mosquitoes, met the requirements of Australia's environmental agencies, and seemed to mollify the angry locals.

The midge, which is more commonly called a no-see-um in the United States, is a tiny black fly that likes to congregate around beaches and lakes, making it a serious irritant for vacationers. (Midges are sometimes called sand flies, but the sand fly is actually quite a different insect.)

"One midge is an entomological curiosity,
a thousand can be hell!"

Biting midges are known as pool feeders. They like to break the skin and simply lap up the blood that seeps out, rather than go to all the work of hunting for a blood vessel. Their bites can cause an allergic reaction that leads to unsightly swollen red bite marks. This reaction is sometimes called sweet itch or, in Australia, Queensland itch. Only the females bite, but the males swarm people constantly, waiting for the females to show up for dinner, giving victims the impression of being constantly under attack.

Campers, beach lovers, and golfers on the Gulf and Atlantic coasts have long suffered through attacks of biting midges during the summer months. In Scotland the so-called Highland midge, *C. impunctatus,* is so aggressive that it deters tourists from hiking or golfing near the country's famous bogs and lakes during the summer. A local pest control company established the Scottish Midge Forecast to help predict midge infestations based on weather conditions and encourage tourists to plan their trips accordingly.

Although midges are not known to transmit human diseases in the United States, in Brazil and around the Amazon both the midge and the mosquito transmit a dengue-like disease called Oropouche fever, which causes severe flu-like symptoms but usually results in full recovery. In some parts of Brazil, up to 44 percent of the population test positive for antibodies to this virus.

A bite from a midge can also deliver a parasitic nematode from the genus *Mansonella;* the tiny worms usually inhabit humans undetected, making diagnosis difficult but also making treatment less urgent. Scientists recently discovered that the nematodes require an abundant supply of bacteria in their own guts; after giving patients in one West African village a round of antibiotics, the bacteria inside the nematodes were killed off and the nematodes then died as well. But because the disease is relatively mild, causing only itching, rashes, and fatigue, it seems unlikely that antibiotics will be distributed on a large scale to rid people of the parasite.

The midge poses a more serious threat to cattle around the world, transmitting a disease called bluetongue that causes a severe fever, swelling of the face and mouth, and the characteristic blue tongue. Thanks to the migration of the biting midge, this disease has spread throughout most of the world, and is gradually moving into more northern climates as the midges themselves move north, perhaps due to climate change.

Meet the Relatives Biting midges are true flies; they are related to black flies, mosquitoes, and other tiny bloodsucking pests. There are about four thousand species of midges worldwide.

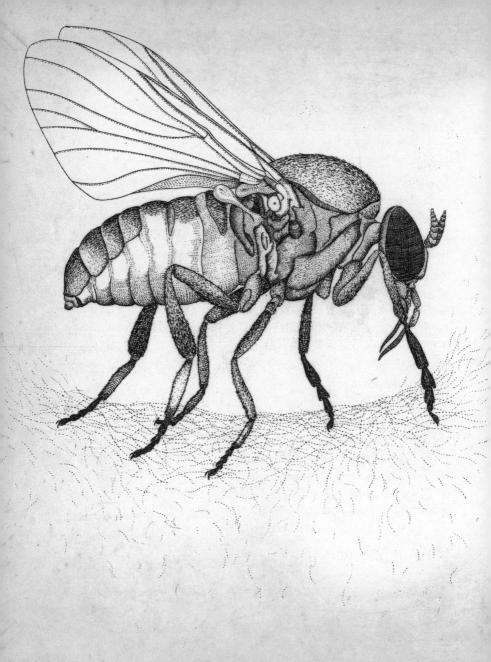

Black Fly

SIMULIUM DAMNOSUM

As recently as the 1970s, a third of villagers living alongside West African rivers could expect to be blind by the time they reached adulthood. Photographs of children leading blind adults around by ropes demonstrated that loss of sight was a normal part of life in these fertile valleys. Eventually those areas had to be abandoned, a terrible decision for people who depended on the rich soil for agriculture. The blame for this tragedy rests with the black fly, called one of "the world's most persistent and demoralizing man-biting insects" by a leading medical entomologist. But the fly alone is not to blame. The bizarre life cycle of a skinny wormlike creature called *Onchocerca volvulus* is the real culprit in the horrific disease known as river blindness, or onchocerciasis.

SIZE:
2–5 mm

FAMILY:
Simuliidae

HABITAT:
Near fast-moving streams

DISTRIBUTION:
Various species are found throughout the United States and Canada, as well as across Europe, Russia, and Africa

Female black flies lay their eggs on the surface of fast-moving rivers, where the water has the high oxygen content their young require. The eggs hatch and the larvae linger along the river for a week before they emerge as fully formed adults. The females mate immediately and only once; after that, they desperately seek out a warm-blooded creature to feed upon. It is only by drinking the blood of a person or an animal that they can get enough nutrition to nurture their eggs along. They will live for a month, laying their eggs in the river to perpetuate the cycle. Some rivers can produce one billion flies per kilometer of riverbed in a single day.

Black flies are "determined feeders," meaning that they anchor themselves and refuse to let go until they are satisfied. A person under attack in an area of heavy infestation might expect to get hundreds of bites in an hour. In some cases the flies swarm so densely, climbing into the ears, nose, eyes, and mouth, that an animal can suffocate or run itself off a cliff in an attempt to get away. The flies have even killed livestock by exsanguination, or the draining of blood. During a massive attack, the shock to the system from the various compounds found in their saliva, a condition called simuliotoxicosis, can also kill an animal in a couple of hours. In 1923, along the Danube River in the southern Carpathian Mountains, a ferocious swarm left twenty-two thousand animals dead.

But the most remarkable fact of the black fly's short, bloodthirsty life is that if it happens to feast upon the blood of a person infected with a parasitic nematode called *Onchocerca volvulus,* it takes part in a weirdly intricate cycle of disease transmission.

The young nematodes—called microfilariae during their early larval stage—cannot grow and develop while they are swimming in the bloodstream of a human. They must be sucked into the body of a black fly while it feeds in order to grow into their next larval stage. Once inside the fly, they move into its saliva and wait for it to feed again—because only by moving back into the body of a human can the worm continue its journey to adulthood.

If they successfully navigate this complicated voyage from human to fly and back to human, the microfilariae finally transform into adult nematodes that can reach over a foot in length. These adults nestle into nodules under a person's skin where they live for up to fifteen years, mating and producing as many as a thousand offspring per day.

In 1923, along the Danube River
in the southern Carpathian Mountains,
a ferocious swarm left twenty-two
thousand animals dead.

And what do those offspring do with their time? Most will never be lucky enough to find their way into the gut of a black fly, as they must do to reach the next developmental stage, which means that they will be doomed to swim around the human body in their juvenile state for a year or two until they die—but not before inflicting terrible symptoms on their host. They burrow into the eyes, where they cause blindness. The skin gets depigmented and breaks out in rashes and lesions. The tiny creatures cause such a horrible itch that people break their skin open with sticks and rocks in a futile attempt to scratch the irritation away. This, in turn, causes bacterial infections, makes it impossible to sleep, and has even driven some poor souls to suicide.

Today 17.7 million people are infected worldwide, primarily in Africa and Latin America. Of those, 270,000 are blind and 500,000 live with severe vision impairment. One approach to controlling the disease is to kill the black fly, and that worked through the 1950s when DDT was available. But the flies became resistant to DDT, and DDT itself accumulated in the food chain at toxic levels. Now a particular strain of a natural bacteria (*Bacillus thuringiensis* var. *israelensis*) is used in its place, but this provides no treatment for the millions affected by the disease.

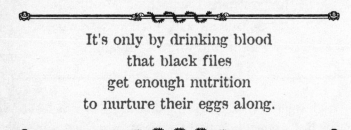

It's only by drinking blood
that black files
get enough nutrition
to nurture their eggs along.

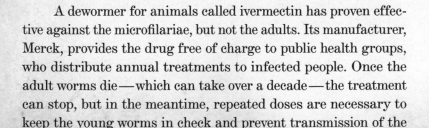

A dewormer for animals called ivermectin has proven effective against the microfilariae, but not the adults. Its manufacturer, Merck, provides the drug free of charge to public health groups, who distribute annual treatments to infected people. Once the adult worms die—which can take over a decade—the treatment can stop, but in the meantime, repeated doses are necessary to keep the young worms in check and prevent transmission of the disease. The program, which was first limited to a few countries in Africa, has been so successful that abandoned river valleys are being resettled and distribution of the drug is beginning in other African and Latin American countries.

Meet the Relatives Although there are over seven hundred species of black fly worldwide, only 10 to 20 percent are pests to humans or animals. They don't all transmit disease, but they are an incredible nuisance, interfering with tourism and outdoor enterprises, like logging and farming, throughout the summer months.

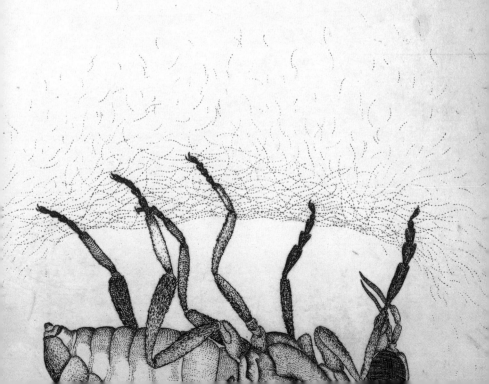

Black Widow

LATRODECTUS HESPERUS

To whom it may concern," wrote twenty-six-year-old Stephen Liarsky in his suicide note. "Whenever a man usually takes his life it is always proper to give the reason. My reason is because, first, I have no job. I have no one in this world except a woman I love terribly, and she is too good for me. I am ashamed of myself because I am a failure and not a success. God bless Rose. Good-bye."

The 1935 suicide was unusual not so much for its motive but for its method: a black widow spider bite. The spider was found in a cardboard box under Mr. Liarsky's bed, along with paperwork indicating that he had purchased her from California and gained assurances that her bite was fatal and incurable.

He died two days later. Hospital officials found a bottle of sleeping pills under his pillow and ruled that the pills, not the spider, were to blame for his death. But it was too late. By that time, the so-called Black Widow Suicide had attracted nationwide attention. Several high-profile reports of black widow deaths started appearing

SIZE:
38 mm (including legs)

FAMILY:
Theridiidae

HABITAT:
Dark, secluded areas, including logs and rock piles, under shrubs and trees, and around woodpiles, sheds, barns, and cellars

DISTRIBUTION:
Nearly worldwide—North and South America, Africa, the Middle East, Europe, Asia, Australia, and New Zealand

in the news. An investigative reporter in Texas tried to prove that suicide by black widow was impossible by attempting (unsuccessfully) to persuade a black widow to bite him. A committee was formed in Oklahoma to eliminate the spider from the state in the name of protecting the children. In 1939 the London Zoo killed its black widow spiders, along with its venomous snakes and insects, as a precaution against the possibility of their being liberated during air raids.

In 1939 the London Zoo killed its black widow spiders, along with its venomous snakes and insects, as a precaution against the possibility of their being liberated during air raids.

The black widow is perhaps the best known and most widely feared spider in the world. About forty species of *Latrodectus* can be found around the world in North and South America, Africa, Australia, and Europe. The female's round, black body is usually (but not always) marked by a distinctive red hourglass shape on the abdomen. The males—small, light brown creatures that bear little resemblance to their wives—don't bite at all, making them more of an afterthought in the story of these frightful creatures.

Although the spider gets its name from the belief that the

females always eat the males after mating, this behavior is seen most often in the Australian species, the redback spider or *Latrodectus hasselti*. The male works so hard to get the female's attention that he will sometimes offer his abdomen up as dinner while he attempts to mate with her. He stands on his head, drapes his abdomen across her mouth, and tries to quickly finish the business of copulation while she coats him in digestive juices and starts to nibble. If he's not fast enough, he will, in fact, die for love.

After a female black widow has mated once, she stores enough sperm to lay eggs for the rest of her life. She'll create a series of egg cases over her one-to-two-year lifespan, filling each one with hundreds of eggs, although only a few dozen may survive to adulthood. Once the young spiderlings are about three weeks old, they perch in their mother's web, waiting for a favorable breeze, then release a thin silk thread that allows them to float away in a process called ballooning. They land where the wind takes them and build their own webs.

Black widows are not particularly eager to bite people; they prefer to use their fangs to go after other insects, which they inject with digestive juices, turning their prey to mush and making it easy to drink them down. If they are provoked into biting a person, they inject a tiny bit of venom under the skin, which may cause a pinprick of pain or no pain at all. It isn't until the venom makes its way to the nervous system that trouble begins. The toxin in a black widow's venom will cause a kind of painful storm in the nervous system, bringing on muscle pain and cramps. People might get shaky and dizzy, and feel their heart race or dangerously slow down. Some people experience sweating, especially around the site of the bite. Doctors call this syndrome latrodectism after the spider's scientific name.

The bite is rarely fatal, but bite victims are encouraged to seek treatment for the symptoms, which can be painful and debilitating. In severe cases, victims may receive an antivenin made from the blood serum of horses that has been injected with black widow venom. This venom can only be obtained by "milking" live black widow spiders, a laborious process that involves giving the spiders a mild electrical shock to induce them to eject venom, which is then vacuumed into a narrow tube. The spider often vomits as a result of the electrical shock, making it necessary to set up a dual vacuum system to separate the vomit from the venom as they spew forth from the spider's mouth.

Black widows do tend to bite when they feel trapped. In the days of outdoor privies, spiders hiding under the toilet seat would attack anything that appeared to block their exit. Fortunately, the introduction of indoor plumbing has made these excruciating bites in the most sensitive of locations a thing of the past.

Meet the Relatives About thirty species of venomous spiders make up the *Latrodectus* genus. They are part of a large and diverse family of spiders known as cobweb or tangle-web spiders.

STINGING CATERPILLARS

A twenty-two-year-old Canadian woman on vacation in Peru returned home to find strange bruises on her legs. For four days she watched as they got bigger, not smaller. She was otherwise in perfect health. Her doctor asked if anything unusual had happened on her vacation, and she said that one week earlier, while walking barefoot in Peru, she had stepped on five caterpillars. The pain had been immediate and severe, running up her thigh and making it painful to walk. She also got a headache. But she felt fine the next day and it didn't occur to her to see a doctor at the time.

After she returned home, the bruises began. Some of them were as large as her hand and getting bigger. Her doctors searched for medical reports of caterpillar stings and realized that a species from Brazil could be to blame. They contacted a hospital there and made arrangements to ship a Brazilian-made antivenin to Canada. It would take two days to arrive.

But on her third day in the hospital—now ten days after the caterpillar sting and within hours of the antivenin's arrival from Brazil—she went into kidney and liver failure. Her blood wasn't clotting properly. By the time the antivenin was administered, multiple organs had failed. She died later that day.

Cases of death by caterpillar are extraordinarily rare and limited to just a few known species, but there are many caterpillars who employ painful defenses to protect themselves.

FIRE CATERPILLAR   *Lonomia obliqua* and *L. achelous*

These are the species most likely to have killed the Canadian woman. *L. obliqua* is found in southern Brazil and *L. achelous* in northern Brazil and Venezuela. The green, brown, and white caterpillars are covered in sharp hairs that resemble tiny cactus spines. They tend to mass together on the ground or on the trunk of a tree, making it possible to be stung by several at once just by walking barefoot or leaning against a tree. The caterpillars release a powerful toxin that causes massive internal bleeding and organ failure. Although the antivenin developed in Brazil is effective, it should be administered within twenty-four hours of the sting, making it critical to seek immediate medical attention.

Brazilian scientists believe that deforestation is bringing more people into contact with the caterpillar. As the jungle trees it prefers get cut down, the caterpillar moves into more populated areas, seeking out fruit trees in orchards as a food source. Over the last decade, public health officials have recorded 444 *Lonomia* stings, 7 of which resulted in death.

GYPSY MOTH CATERPILLAR *Lymantria dispar*

An invasive European moth was to blame for a series of mysterious rashes among schoolchildren in northern Pennsylvania. In the spring of 1981, roughly a third of the children at two schools in Luzerne County suffered from rashes on their arms, necks, and legs. Doctors took scrapings and throat cultures to test for infection, but found nothing. Finally they pulled aside children who didn't have a rash and interviewed them about the amount of time they spent playing outside in the woods. They asked the same questions to the children with the rashes and found a high correlation between outdoor play and the outbreak of this mysterious rash. They concluded that the rash had been caused by the gypsy moth caterpillar, which was present in high concentrations in the woods around those two schools.

The rash caused by the long, silky hairs of this caterpillar can be painful, but isn't known to inflict long-term harm. However, the caterpillars do significant damage to forests. In the last thirty years, over a million acres of hardword forests have been defoliated annually. While the caterpillars may not kill the trees, they weaken them enough to allow diseases to take hold. The caterpillar, and its adult form, the gypsy moth, are both found in Canada, along the east coast of the United States, and as far west as Michigan, Ohio, Minnesota, Illinois, Washington, and Oregon.

ARCHDUKE CATERPILLAR
Lexias spp

These beautiful Southeast Asian butterflies are often found in butterfly conservatories and framed butterfly collections. The wings of the
adult males are primarily black with patterns of blue, yellow, or white
markings. The pale green caterpillars, rarely seen except in their native countries or on butterfly farms, are covered with exquisitely sharp
spines that extend outward like the needles of a pine tree. This thorny
armor deters predators and protects the young caterpillars from getting
eaten by their siblings as they search for food.

PUSS CATERPILLAR
Megalopyge opercularis

Don't be fooled by the fact that this caterpillar looks just like a tiny Persian cat. The so-called flannel moth or asp moth is one of the most toxic
caterpillars in North America. Anyone who rubs up against its long,
silky golden-brown hairs will find those hairs embedded under the skin,
where they cause severe burning pain, a rash, and blisters. The pain can
radiate up the limb, and the most extreme reactions can also include
nausea, swollen lymph nodes, and respiratory distress. Most people recover in a day, but in the worst cases it may take several days for symptoms to subside. People who have been stung say that the pain felt like
a broken arm or being hit with a hammer. The pain is so intense and
unexpected that some people also suffer panic attacks.

There is no specific treatment, other than ice packs, antihistamines,
or creams and ointments to soothe the pain. The hairs can sometimes
be pulled out by applying tape to the skin, but even this may offer little
relief. The caterpillars are found throughout the southern United States
in late spring and early summer. The adults, which emerge later in the
summer, are also extremely fuzzy, resembling a large, furry bee.

IO MOTH CATERPILLAR   *Automeris io*

The io moth is a familiar creature in its native range, which extends from southern Ontario, Quebec, and New Brunswick down through North and South Dakota, into Arizona, New Mexico, and Texas, and east to Florida. The moths have large spots resembling eyes on their lower wings, making them a popular subject for nature photographers. But the caterpillars are fascinating as well—and fearsome. These pale green creatures are covered with fleshy nodules, and from each nodule sprouts a cluster of stinging, black-tipped spines. The sting is painful but harmless, although allergic reactions can be severe and may require medical attention.

Don't be fooled by the fact that this caterpillar
looks just like a tiny Persian cat.

SADDLEBACK CATERPILLAR   *Acharia stimulea*

This short, fat, brown caterpillar has a distinctive green "saddle" that runs across the middle of its back and down the sides, with a dark purple spot in the center. This creature sports groups of spines that protect its head, rear end, and the sides of its abdomen. The sting is usually described as being similar to a bee sting. The saddleback is found throughout the southern United States in spring, and the dark brown adult moth can be seen flying in July and August.

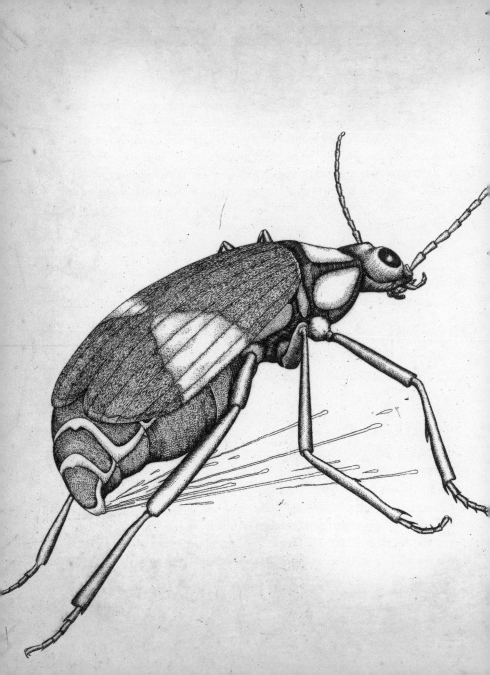

Bombardier Beetle

STENAPTINUS INSIGNIS

When Charles Darwin was a young man at Cambridge in 1828, he found his passion not in the classroom, but in the outdoors. Like many young Englishmen of his day, he was an avid beetle collector. Hunting for bugs in the English countryside might seem like a fairly tame pastime, but Darwin managed to get into trouble—and make an interesting discovery—during one of his field trips.

"One day," he wrote, "on tearing off some old bark, I saw two rare beetles, and seized one in each hand; then I saw a third and new kind, which I could not bear to lose, so that I popped the one which I held in my right hand into my mouth. Alas! it ejected some intensely acrid fluid, which burnt my tongue so that I was forced to spit the beetle out, which was lost, as was the third one."

The beetle Darwin placed in his mouth was almost certainly a kind of ground beetle known as a bombardier beetle. Grab one of these insects and you'll hear a surprisingly loud popping noise just as a hot, stinging spray is ejected from an artillery-like structure on the bug's rear end.

SIZE:
Up to 20 mm

FAMILY:
Carabidae

HABITAT:
Bombardier beetles live in a variety of habitats, from deserts to forests

DISTRIBUTION:
North and South America, Europe, Australia, Middle East, Africa, Asia, New Zealand

With the possible exception of flustered collectors who store live insects in their mouths for safekeeping, the bombardier beetle poses little threat to humans. However, its enemies—ants, larger beetles, spiders, even frogs and birds—flee in terror when the bombardier takes aim.

The insect fires repeatedly, like an automatic weapon, ejecting five hundred to one thousand blasts per second at its attacker.

The mechanism by which it engages its enemy would fascinate any weapons manufacturer. In one gland the bombardier stores hydroquinones, a precursor to the very irritating chemical compound 1,4-benzoquinone that it sprays at its enemies. Also in that gland is hydrogen peroxide. The two don't interact unless they are mixed with a catalyst—and that is exactly what happens when the bombardier comes under attack. The contents of the reservoir are forced into a reaction chamber and mixed with a catalyst that transforms the chemicals and heats them to the boiling point. The reaction creates enough pressure to force the spray out of the reaction chamber with a loud pop. Sophisticated recordings of this phenomenon show that the insect fires repeatedly, like an automatic weapon, ejecting five hundred to one thousand blasts per second at its attacker.

Ironically, the beetle that attacked Charles Darwin has since been used to attack his theory of evolution. Creationists and advocates of intelligent design claim that the beetle's defense mechanism is too complex to have evolved gradually. Instead, they claim, the system of chambers is "irreducibly complex," meaning that the individual parts could not possibly have evolved separately through genetic mutation to function together in such an extraordinarily sophisticated manner. One oft-repeated but erroneous claim is that the hydrogen peroxide and hydroquinones are stored separately in the bug's body, and that if they were mixed, the bug would explode, making it impossible that the chambers could have evolved over time. Entomologists have pointed out the error in this description of the bug's anatomy; in fact, they are stored together and mixed with a catalyst before firing. They also point out that the various elements of the beetle's firepower are already present across many species, making its powerful weaponry less improbable than it may seem.

About five hundred species of bombardier beetles are found under boards, bark, and loose rocks throughout the world. At night they scramble about in the open, preferring damp areas. Thanks to their elegant defense system, some can live for several years. The African bombardier beetle, *Stenaptinus insignis,* is impressive not only for its bright yellow and black markings but also for its ability to swivel its hindquarters up to 270 degrees, allowing it to spray in almost any direction and knock an attacker off its back.

Meet the Relatives There are over three thousand species in this family, found worldwide.

Brazilian Wandering Spider

PHONEUTRIA SP.

It was a normal day at the Rio de Janeiro airport. Luggage rolled smoothly through the security checkpoint, the X-ray machines revealing the usual assortment of bikinis and sandals and suntan lotion. But the contents of one suitcase brought the entire checkpoint to a halt. Judging from the image on the X-ray machine, the suitcase appeared to hold hundreds of tiny, twisted legs.

Someone was trying to sneak deadly spiders out of Brazil. The suitcase was carefully packed with tiny white boxes, each one holding a single live spider. The smuggler was a young Welshman who claimed he was bringing them back to Wales to sell in his spider shop. A complete search of his luggage turned up one thousand spiders in all. He even packed them in his carry-on bag, leading Brazilian security officials to remark that had the spiders escaped and starting dropping down from the overhead bins during the flight, the chaos would have been unimaginable.

SIZE:
150 mm, including legs

FAMILY:
Ctenidae

HABITAT:
Jungles, rain forests, and dark, secluded areas like woodpiles and sheds

DISTRIBUTION:
Central and South America

The spiders were sent to a laboratory for identification, where it became clear that these were no ordinary arachnids: one of the species the Welshman had collected was the Brazilian wandering spider, believed to be among the most dangerous in the world.

This large, grayish brown spider is unusual in that it doesn't spin a web and wait for prey to blunder into it. Instead, it prowls the floor of the jungle and even walks through the city, hunting for dinner late into the night. And while most spiders will scurry away at the sight of an aggressor, the Brazilian wandering spider stands its ground, rising up on its hind legs, ready for a fight. Anyone who swats at one of these spiders had better aim to kill, because if it survives a swat with a broom it might try to climb straight up the handle and bite.

Had the spiders escaped and starting dropping down from the overhead bins during the flight, the chaos would have been unimaginable.

The bite causes a flood of immediate and severe pain, which can be followed by difficulty breathing, paralysis, and even asphyxiation. One of the stranger symptoms of this spider's bite is priapism, a persistent erection. Unfortunately, it's not a sign of arousal but of severe envenomation. People who suspect that they've been bitten by a Brazilian wandering spider must seek immediate medical attention, but with proper care and a little luck they will survive.

There are eight species of wandering spiders in the *Phoneutria* genus, all found throughout parts of Central and South America and recognizable for their eight eyes, four of which form a box shape directly in the front of their face. The eight species are not all equally venomous, and most people who are bitten suffer only mild pain and recover fully. However, the most venomous species are capable of killing, with young children and the elderly at the greatest risk.

Because it sometimes climbs around in banana trees hunting for prey, the spider can end up as a stowaway in shipments of bananas, earning it the nickname "banana spider." There are many harmless look-alike species that turn up in bananas and other cargo as well, and only a few scientists around the world are capable of making an accurate identification. It is difficult, therefore, to rely on media accounts of *Phoneutria* bites inflicted by spiders in imported produce. Nonetheless, a British chef unpacking a box of bananas in the kitchen was reportedly bitten by one in 2005; in spite of the pain and shock, he managed to grab his cell phone and snap a picture of the spider. The spider itself was later found in the kitchen, allowing experts to identify it and give the man the right course of treatment. He survived, but only after spending a week in the hospital.

Meet the Relatives Other members of the Ctenidae family are generally ground-dwelling spiders that hunt rather than spin webs, but less is known about the potency of their venom.

CURSE OF THE SCORPION

A scorpion bite may be painful, but it's almost never fatal—for adults. Children are another matter. A California family vacationing in Puerto Vallarta in 1994 learned this the hard way, when their thirteen-month-old child stepped on a scorpion that had been hiding in his shoe. The boy started crying and frothing at the mouth and soon developed a high fever. At a local emergency room he stopped breathing a few times. Finally his parents called a San Diego hospital and had him flown there, where he was placed on life support. He did survive, but even hospital staff weren't sure he would make it.

In a small child, the neurotoxic venom of a scorpion can cause seizures, loss of muscle control, and unbearable pain all over the body as it goes to work on the nerves. Until recently, parents had to watch helplessly as doctors did what little they could to manage the symptoms and sedate the child as the venom spread through the body.

Fortunately, a new treatment is in clinical trials now. At the Phoenix Children's Hospital, parents are offered the choice of sedation for their child, or a new antivenin called Anascorp. The drug is administered intravenously and starts working within a couple of hours, usually allowing the victim to go home with pain medications that

day. This breakthrough is being cheered in Arizona, where eight thousand people are stung every year, two hundred of them small children who suffer serious side effects.

Scorpions are found in desert, tropical, and subtropical areas throughout the world, and over twelve hundred species of these arachnids have been identified. As with spider bites, it is often difficult to prove that a particular species is responsible for a sting, unless the scorpion is captured and identified. But here are just a few to avoid:

ARIZONA BARK SCORPION
Centruroides sculpturatus

This is the scorpion most feared by Arizonans. It lives in the southwestern United States and in Mexico, nestling under rocks and piles of wood, but also making its way into homes. At only seven to eight centimeters in length, it is easy to miss, especially as it is active at night. Fortunately, scorpions glow under ultraviolet light, so Arizonans who wish to check for scorpions before they go to bed can use a blacklight flashlight, which is often marketed as a scorpion-hunting tool. The sting is considered to be the most painful of any scorpion in the United States, lasting for up to seventy-two hours and potentially dangerous to pets and small children. A related species, the Durango scorpion *Centruroides suffusus,* is found in the Chihuahuan desert and is one of the deadliest scorpions in Mexico.

FATTAIL SCORPION
Androctonus crassicauda

Soldiers in Iraq are warned to watch out for this highly dangerous dark brown scorpion, which gets its name from its menacing, oversized tail. The military classifies it as one of the deadliest scorpions in the world and warns that it can cause death by heart or respiratory failure.

DEATHSTALKER
Leiurus quinquestriatus

Another Middle Eastern scorpion that soldiers are warned to avoid, this light yellow and beige scorpion is easy to overlook in sandy soil, but its venom is highly toxic. An Air Force medic who was stung twice had to be flown to a hospital, where she was put on life support and given an experimental antivenin to save her life.

Scorpions glow under ultraviolet light, so Arizonans who wish to check under their beds for scorpions can use a blacklight flashlight.

TRINIDAD SCORPION
Tityus trinitatis

Found around Trinidad and in Venezuela, these diminutive creatures reach only five to six centimeters in length but deliver a painful sting that can cause pancreatitis. The deaths of a few children have been attributed to the venom of this scorpion, usually due to damage to the myocardium, or heart muscle.

WHIP SCORPION
Mastigoproctus giganteus

While not a true scorpion, this arachnid, also called a vinegarroon, uses an extraordinary piece of natural artillery to defend itself: rather than sting its enemy, it sprays a liquid made of 84 percent acetic acid. Household vinegar is only 5 percent acetic acid, making this something like the strongest vinegar imaginable. What is most extraordinary about this defense is the fact that it can whip its tail around and spray in any direction, sending predators running for cover.

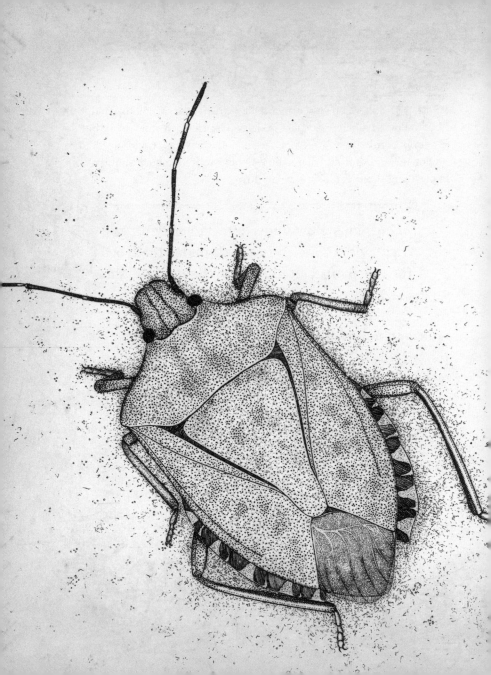

Brown Marmorated Stink Bug

HALYOMORPHA HALYS

Some residents of Pennsylvania and New Jersey dread the arrival of autumn, because it means the beginning of the annual invasion of flattened, grayish-brown insects from China. They crawl in the tiniest hole, able to gain entry through cracks around doors and windows, crevices in the attic, and ductwork. They make themselves at home, glad to be away from the winter's chill and ready to spend the next several months enjoying indoor life.

One family in Lower Allen Township, Pennsylvania, complained that when they opened kitchen cabinets, the bugs were sitting in their dishes. They found them waiting inside drawers and under the bed and crawling through the attic by the hundreds. And when Christmas came, the bugs climbed up the family's tree and took their place among the ornaments.

The husband, who suffers from obsessive compulsive disorder, couldn't stand the sight of the bugs. He stretched duct tape around his windows, but they kept coming back. Even going to

SIZE:
17 mm

FAMILY:
Pentatomidae

HABITAT:
Orchards, agricultural fields, meadows

DISTRIBUTION:
China, Japan, Taiwan, Korea, and parts of the United States

65

work offered no respite: as a mailman, he found them in mail-boxes all day long.

What makes these home invaders so intolerable is their smell. It is difficult to describe the odor of a stink bug; some people characterize it as a rotten fruit smell, a combination of cherries and grass, or a moldy, musky almond fragrance. Most people simply call it a foul, heinous odor that they'll never forget. Disturbing the bugs, stepping on them, or vacuuming them up—the control method recommended by experts—releases the stink, which in turn can function as a kind of signal to attract more stink bugs to the home. In large quantities, some species have even created traffic hazards: in 1905, newly installed electrical lights drew so many stink bugs to intersections in Phoenix that street cars couldn't plough through the piles of bugs massed on the ground.

When Christmas came, the bugs climbed up the family's tree and took their place among the ornaments.

The brown marmorated stink bug was probably introduced to Pennsylvania by accident in the late 1990s. Like other stink bugs or shield insects in the Pentatomidae family, these wide, flat insects look like a shield when viewed from above. Their defensive secretions contain cyanide, which explains the bitter almond smell. And while stink bugs are generally harmless, inflicting only minimal damage to plants, this Asian invader is being watched closely as it has the potential to become a pest of fruit trees, soybeans, and other crops. After establishing itself in Pennsylvania, it moved into New Jersey and then showed up across the country in Oregon. It has now been seen in twenty-seven states.

While its damage to plants has been mild so far, the stink bug is universally despised as an indoor pest. It crawls around in closets, requiring people to shake out their clothes before getting dressed. Women find the bugs crawling in their hair. They creep in through window-mounted air conditioning units, making it necessary to remove the units or seal them completely during winter months. While pyrethroid insecticides sprayed around a home's exterior in the fall might keep them out, they are of little use against the bugs indoors and may pose more health hazards than the bugs themselves. Vacuuming up the bugs does work, but the stink is so powerful that most people buy a separate vacuum cleaner just for bug removal.

One small comfort is that the bugs don't breed in the winter, so they don't start new families indoors. Once spring arrives, the adults leave of their own accord to return to gardens and fields, where they will mate and lay eggs. The eggs hatch in late summer, and the nymphs go through five stages of molting before reaching adulthood. This new generation then goes in search of a place to spend the winter, settling indoors by October, just as their parents did.

Meet the Relatives Stink bugs are a large and diverse family found in Australia, North America, Europe, Asia, Africa, and South America. Relations include the leaf-footed bugs, which feed on a wide variety of plants.

Brown Recluse

LOXOSCELES RECLUSA

Ah, the poor, misunderstood brown recluse. This unassuming spider gets blamed for every kind of pustule, boil, and eruption that might afflict a person. According to reports in medical journals, the brown recluse has been held responsible for staphylococcus infections, herpes, shingles, lymphoma, diabetes-related ulcers, chemical burns, and even allergic reactions to prescription medications. Arachnologists insist that there are only two ways to accurately diagnose a brown recluse bite: to either capture the spider in the act and get it identified or have a dermatologist biopsy a fresh bite wound. Without that evidence, it is entirely likely that the painful, rotting lesion that sends a person running to the doctor was caused by something other than this dreaded spider—and the misdiagnosis is often more deadly than the spider bite itself.

SIZE:
Up to 9.5 mm

FAMILY:
Sicariidae

HABITAT:
Dry, sheltered, undisturbed places like woodpiles, sheds, and undergrowth

DISTRIBUTION:
Central and southern United States

That's not to say that the brown recluse doesn't bite, or that its bite isn't painful. A severe brown recluse bite manifests itself as a nasty, swollen skin ulcer with dead tissue in the center. These bites form a red, white, and blue bulls-eye pattern, with a painful red area around the edge, then a white circle where blood flow is restricted, then a bluish-gray spot in the center that represents

69

dying flesh. Contrary to rumors, most people recover from these wounds quickly, with only the more severe cases lasting a month or two. While there have been news reports of deaths caused by brown recluse bites, these accounts are disputed by some of the nation's leading brown recluse experts.

A Kansas family collected over two thousand brown recluse spiders in and around their home. Remarkably, no one was bitten.

What accounts for the number of misdiagnosed brown recluse bites? The spider itself was virtually unknown until the second half of the twentieth century, when a handful of news accounts placed the blame for mysterious wounds with this little-known spider. Now it seems that every person with an unexplained sore is able to find a small brown spider nearby. The brown recluse is easily confused with other species: similar arachnids resemble it and several even have the same violin-shaped marking on the back. The only way to accurately identify a brown recluse is to look deep into its eyes: they have six of them, arranged in three pairs. Experts also look for a uniformly brown abdomen covered in fine hairs; brown, smooth legs; and a small size (the body no more than nine and a half millimeters long).

Spiders in the genus *Loxosceles* are found in central and southern areas of the United States, but reports of their bites persist nationwide. To date, *L. reclusa* has only been positively identified in sixteen states: Texas, Oklahoma, Kansas, Missouri, Arkansas, Louisiana, Mississippi, Alabama, Tennessee, Kentucky, and parts of neighboring states, including Nebraska, Iowa, Illinois, Indiana, Ohio, and Georgia. A few other species, including *L. deserta, arizonica, apachea, blanda,* and *devia,* have been found along the Mexico border through Texas, New Mexico, Arizona, and inland portions of southern California, but none of these are the true brown recluse.

Reports of the spider in other parts of the country are so persistent that frustrated arachnologists have offered rewards to anyone who could send them an actual brown recluse from an area where they are not known to live. One California scientist called it the "Show Me the Spider" challenge. After years of attempting to locate a brown recluse in the state, University of California entomologists have declared that the brown recluse definitively does not live in California.

For people who do live in places where the spider is found, it can be disturbing to realize how many of them live nearby. A family in Kansas collected over two thousand brown recluse spiders in and around their home in just six months. Remarkably, no one was bitten in the six years they lived in the house. A recluse usually won't bite unless it is quite literally forced against the skin. For this reason, the best advice experts can offer is to shake out camping gear, as well as bedding or clothing that's been in storage or crumpled on the floor for a long period of time. Avoid the recluse, they say, and the recluse will avoid you.

Meet the Relatives Recluse spiders are related to another genus of six-eyed spiders called the six-eyed sand spider. These spiders are known for their necrotic venom.

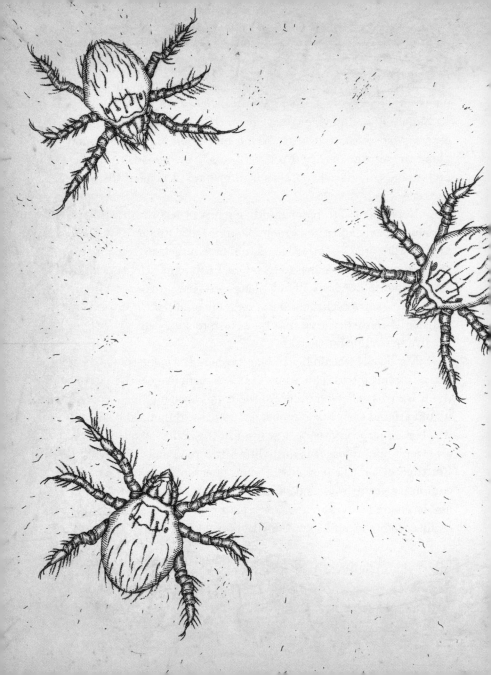

Chigger Mite

LEPTOTROMBIDIUM SP.

Soldiers fighting in World War II had to face down more than the enemy. In Burma, monsoon weather, unfamiliar terrain, and exotic diseases made for a deadly combination. Virtually every soldier in the area was hospitalized at some point during 1944. Although combat was heavy, soldiers were nineteen times more likely to die from disease than from battle wounds. Hepatitis, malaria, dysentery, and venereal diseases posed serious problems, but perhaps the most challenging disease was the unfamiliar and unpredictable scrub typhus, transmitted by a tiny arachnid known as a chigger mite.

The chigger, actually the larval form of a mite in the genus *Leptotrombidium,* is a minute creature that feeds on blood only once in its life. It is so small that its mouth can't even penetrate the skin deeply enough to hit a blood vessel; for this reason it simply bites into the skin and drinks down a kind of liquefied beverage of skin tissue and blood. A person might not even feel the bite until later, when a little redness develops at the site. This is usually caused by the chigger leav-

SIZE:
0.4 mm

FAMILY:
Trombiculidae

HABITAT:
Low-lying, damp grasslands and woodlands

DISTRIBUTION:
Throughout Asia and Australia

ing its feeding tube behind, which can irritate the skin the way a tiny splinter would. Once the chigger has enjoyed its one and only blood meal, it matures into an adult mite and feeds only on plants for the rest of its life.

One Army medical expert predicted that all of his patients infected with scrub typhus would live with permanent heart damage.

How, then, is the chigger mite able to transmit disease? If it only feeds once, there is no opportunity to take up the infection from one host and pass it on to another. Scientists solved this mystery when they were able to prove in the laboratory that these mites are capable of transovarial transmission. In other words, adult chiggers who get infected during their one blood meal then pass the infection on to their offspring. For that reason, a young chigger might already be infected from birth, and pass the infection on when it takes its first and only blood meal.

Scrub typhus, also called tsutsugamushi fever, is found in populations of wild rats, voles, mice, birds, and also in humans. People who have been infected with the *Orientia tsutsugamushi* bacteria usually experience flu-like symptoms after about ten days, including muscle aches, swollen lymph nodes, fever, and loss of appetite. Eventually, the disease can move into the heart, lungs, and kidneys, resulting in death if antibiotics and other life-saving treatments are not administered in time. Up to a third of people who don't get treatment will die from the disease.

During World War II, scrub typhus was frustratingly hard to avoid. The mites lived in tall kunai grass, which grows to ten to twenty feet, and soldiers had no choice but to march through it. Burning down the fields of grass might have eliminated the mites, but this wasn't always feasible in a war zone. The clothing the soldiers wore could hardly be sealed tightly enough to keep these tiny mites away. Soldiers who came down with the disease lost, on average, a hundred days of combat duty, as compared to only fourteen days for malaria cases. Twenty percent of them developed pneumonia, and one Army medical expert who treated the disease predicted that all of his patients infected with scrub typhus would live with permanent heart damage.

Today scrub typhus infections still occur in parts of Australia, Japan, China, Southeast Asia, the Pacific Islands, and Sri Lanka. There is no vaccine available, and over a million people are infected worldwide.

Meet the Relatives Members of this family include harvest mites and other tiny bloodsucking creatures. The larvae of many species of mites may be referred to as chiggers, but the so-called chiggers found in the United States are usually young harvest mites that do not transmit disease.

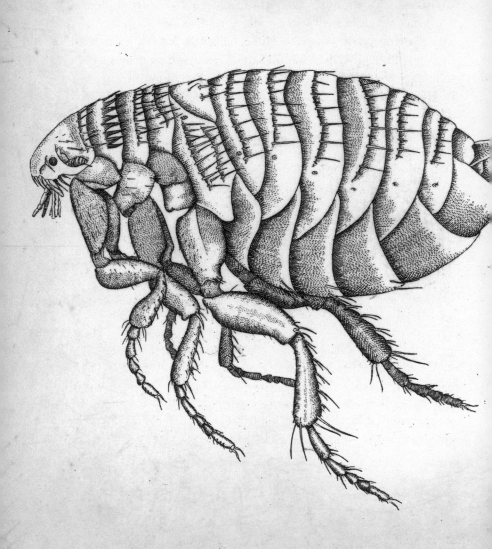

Chigoe Flea

TUNGA PENETRANS

On Christopher Columbus's second voyage to the New World, he established a colony on the island of Hispaniola, which is now home to Haiti and the Dominican Republic. Among the many problems he and his crew faced—a lack of supplies, food shortages, and battles with the local population—nothing was as troublesome as one small sand flea.

Francisco de Oviedo, discussing Columbus's voyages some thirty years later, wrote: "There were two plagues that the Spaniards and new settlers of these Indies suffered, which are natural plagues of this land. The first is syphilis, which was transferred and carried to Spain and from there to other parts of the world . . . and the other is the chigoe." He went on to explain, with surprising accuracy for a sixteenth-century naturalist, the way the flea burrowed under toenails and laid its eggs there, creating what he described as "a small sack the size of a lentil, and sometimes like a garbanzo." He noted that, while it was possible to evict the fleas with a fine needle, "many lost their feet because of the chigoe. Or at least a few toes . . . because it was necessary to cure themselves with iron or fire." We can only as-

SIZE:
1 mm

FAMILY:
Tungidae

HABITAT:
Favors sandy, warm soil on deserts and beaches

DISTRIBUTION:
Tropical regions around the world, including Latin America, India, Africa, and the Caribbean

sume that he meant that Columbus's crew cut off their own toes, so desperate were they to rid themselves of this terrible infestation. Although early treatment with a sterile needle should have been simple, Oviedo wrote that "in the end, the Spaniards were not successful at this, any more than they were at curing syphilis."

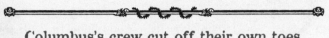

Columbus's crew cut off their own toes,
so desperate were they to rid themselves
of this terrible infestation.

A female chigoe flea burrows into the skin of her host by simply tearing into it, living under the skin and dining on the host's blood until she swells to about the size of a pea. She does not allow her host's skin to heal over, maintaining an open wound so that she can breathe and also so she can receive male visitors when she's feeling amorous. Sometimes her rear end can be seen in the center of the wound as a tiny black dot. She lays about a hundred eggs over the next week or two, and while those eggs are destined for the sandy beach the flea came from, they tend to stick to the wound, making for a truly appalling sight: clusters of tiny white eggs clinging to festering wounds. If left untreated, the eggs will eventually drop to the ground, and after the female has been in residence for about a month, she will die and fall out of the wound as well—but not before creating serious problems for the host.

Tourists who get infested with the flea on some tropical beach usually do not experience this entire life cycle. They notice a lesion on their foot and get right to a doctor, where it can be carefully cleaned up, and the flea removed, before eggs are laid. But in poorer communities, people may live with dozens of these lesions on their feet, resulting in chronic infections, gangrene, and even the loss of toes. Because the fleas infest both people and animals, people who live in close contact with rodents or livestock face far more infestations than tourists strolling on the beach.

One recent study at a favela in northeast Brazil showed that about a third of the community was infested with the fleas, a condition called tungiasis. Some people had over a hundred lesions on their feet, hands, and chest. The infestations were so bad that many of them had trouble walking or gripping anything with their hands. They had lost fingernails and toenails entirely. The researchers made a point of mentioning that local doctors did not observe or treat parasites like the chigoe flea unless they were specifically asked about it. While the idea of a doctor overlooking dozens of sores oozing the eggs of parasites seems impossible, it demonstrates how common the infestation is.

Treatment for people participating in the study consisted of a simple cleaning, a tube of ointment, and the gift of a pair of tennis shoes to each patient—with a strong recommendation that they wear them.

Meet the Relatives Related to other tiny fleas that infest birds and mammals, primarily in South America.

HAVE NO FEAR

Entomologists Robert Coulson and John Witter analyzed the ways in which people respond to insects when they are out in nature. They described five different responses:

Dead Insect Syndrome, in which people respond to insects almost automatically by killing them, especially around campgrounds or picnic tables.

Perfect Leaf Syndrome, in which hikers and campers alert park managers if they see the smallest nibble in a leaf or a tree. (Given the fact that most insects must eat plants in order to survive, such bites are normal and expected.)

Entomophobia, an irrational fear of insects that can cause people to avoid all contact with nature.

No Reaction, a response from people who understand that bugs are part of outdoor life and should be tolerated.

Environmentalist Response, in which people believe that insecticides should not be used in any situation and favor the protection of all bugs under all circumstances.

Of these responses, entomophobia may be the most familiar to us. Most of us know what an attack of irrational fear feels like: dizziness, sweaty palms, tunnel vision, fluttering heart. An extreme phobia can bring on debilitating panic attacks. When it comes to a fear of bugs—who tend to show up unexpectedly and in the most unlikely of places—a phobia may also send people running out of the room, shrieking in terror. Worse, it can drive people to indiscriminate pesticide use, which often poses a far greater threat to human health than would the bugs they are eradicating.

But car accidents? A British insurance company conducted a study in 2008 that showed that over half a million English drivers have had a car accident caused by a bug (or, more precisely, caused by the distraction of a bug in the car). Three percent of drivers surveyed said they never drove with their windows down for fear that a bug might fly in. The insurance company is developing a type of netting that could be stretched over car windows to keep bugs out.

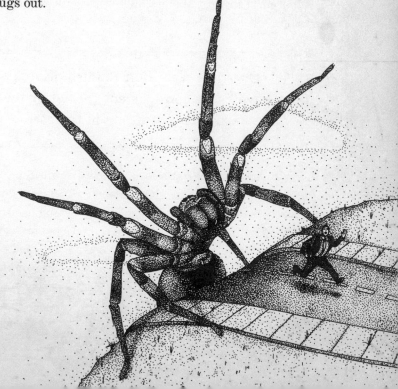

Psychologists help people overcome their phobias by a slow and careful process of desensitization. For an insect phobia, it might begin with a person drawing a picture of a bug. Over a few sessions, they might make that picture more and more lifelike, and eventually work up to looking at a photograph of the creature they fear. Then they might view a dead bug in a jar from across the room, moving gradually closer to it. Once it's possible to look closely at the dead bug without panicking, a live bug might be placed in the jar instead. The more successful patients will eventually be able to tolerate the presence of a live bug walking across a table, and might even be able to have a conversation about the fact that most insects, spiders, and other creepy and slimy creatures pose little real threat.

Over half a million English drivers
have had a car accident caused by the
distraction of a bug in the car.

But perhaps the first step is to identify the fear. The naming of a phobia is more art than science; psychologists only officially recognize phobias as a broad category and use the term to relate to any number of persistent and irrational fears. The practice of attaching a Greek or Latin word to "phobia" to create a more specific name for a particular fear was common in the nineteenth century but is not formally in use by psychologists today.

Here are just a few of the terms that have been invented to describe a fear of bugs:

Acarophobia	Fear of mites or scabies
Apiphobia	Fear of bees
Arachnophobia	Fear of spiders
Cnidophobia	Fear of stings
Delusional parasitosis	Mistaken belief of infestation by parasites
Entomophobia	Fear of insects
Helminthophobia	Fear of being infested with worms
Isopterophobia	Fear of insects that eat wood
Katsaridaphobia	Fear of cockroaches
Lepidopterophobia	Fear of butterflies
Myrmecophobia	Fear of ants
Parasitophobia	Fear of parasites
Pediculophobia	Fear of lice
Scoleciphobia	Fear of parasitic worms
Spheksophobia	Fear of wasps

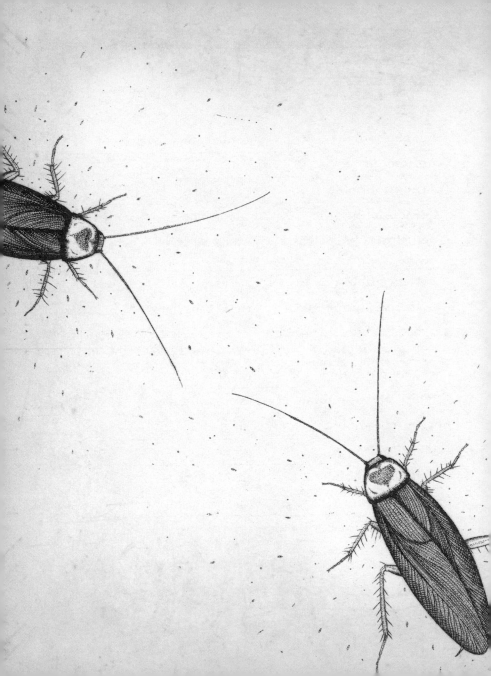

Cockroach

BLATTELLA GERMANICA

The Carmelitos Housing Project in Southern California opened to great fanfare in 1940. A band played "The Star Spangled Banner," a flag was raised, and speeches were given extolling the virtues of this "new design for living." An article written by a new resident proclaimed "Uncle Sam is my landlord!" It was not your typical housing project—the small townhouse-style apartments, each with their own patch of lawn, looked more like vacation bungalows than low-income housing for the poor. This enormous complex—712 apartments in all—was one of the first of its kind to offer people a way out of the depths of the Great Depression.

Twenty years later, health officials noticed a disturbing pattern emerging from the sprawling development: almost 40 percent of all hepatitis A cases in the community came from the Carmelitos Housing Project. At the time, a team of UCLA scientists happened to be testing a new, relatively safe insecticide they had developed called "Dri-die," a silica dust that broke down the waxy cuticle on a cockroach's body, causing it to dry up and die. The UCLA

SIZE:
Up to 15 mm

FAMILY:
Blattellidae

HABITAT:
Lives primarily around humans in homes and buildings

DISTRIBUTION:
Worldwide

team tested their new insecticide at Carmelitos with astonishing results: 70 percent of cockroaches were killed. And while hepatitis A cases continued to increase in the surrounding community, they were almost completely eliminated at Carmelitos. Getting rid of the cockroaches saved the residents from a terrible disease.

"Cockroaches are among the most dreaded of insects," said UCLA's I. Barry Tarshis when he announced the results. "But this has been because they are so associated with filth, hard to get rid of, and look repugnant. Now we have evidence the disgust people feel for them is more than a mere prejudice."

Before this study, there was little evidence to show that cockroaches transmit disease. Today public health officials know that because cockroaches live in and around human habitation and exhibit "communicative behavior"—meaning that they move between filth or contamination and human foods—they can transmit disease.

As one of the oldest insects on the planet, dating back 350 million years, cockroaches have long been associated with humans. But, in fact, of four thousand known species, 95 percent of them live entirely apart from humans, in forests, under logs, in caves, under rocks in the desert, and in damp, dark habitats near lakes and rivers. The 5 percent that do live around people seem to be universally loathed, for any number of reasons.

Cockroaches have no trouble finding their way into any house. They do have wings and some species are capable of short flights; they are known to land on a door and wait until it opens to get inside or to crawl in through any crack or opening. Whether they stay depends entirely upon housekeeping. They love a messy kitchen and bathroom, and once they're in an apartment complex, the shared ductwork, sewer lines, and electrical wiring in multiple dwellings mean that they can easily travel from one to the next without ever going outside. One study showed that roaches in Arizona moved several hundred yards through sewer systems to enter a home. Once inside, cockroaches give off a telltale repulsive, musty odor.

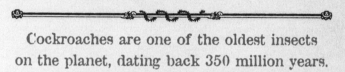

Cockroaches are one of the oldest insects on the planet, dating back 350 million years.

They are omnivorous feeders with what scientists call "unspecialized chewing mouthparts" that make it easy for them to live alongside humans and feed off a wide variety of human waste. Spilled food, trash, and sewage all attract cockroaches, but they will even chew on book bindings and the paste on stamps. Although they don't bite humans, medical entomologists have reported that they feed on "fingernails, eyelashes, skin, calluses of hands and feet, and food residues about the faces of sleeping humans."

All this shuttling between people, food, and garbage mean that roaches carry any number of pathogens around with them, including *E. coli,* salmonella, leprosy, typhoid, dysentery, plague,

hookworm, hepatitis, staphylococcus, and strep-
tococcus. When cockroaches feed, they often
regurgitate a little food from their crop, leaving behind bits of their last meal as they eat
the next one. They also defecate as they move
and feed, depositing tiny brown droppings as
small as flakes of pepper, all of which makes
it easier to spread disease.

If that isn't bad enough, half of all people
with asthma are allergic to cockroaches. Ten percent of nonallergic people also have some kind of
sensitivity to cockroaches, with the most severe reactions causing
anaphylactic shock. Roach allergens can survive the most thor-
ough cleaning measures, including boiling water, changes to pH,
and ultraviolet light. Curiously, a cockroach allergy can bring on
cross-reactions to crab, lobster, shrimp, and crawfish, as well as
dust mites and other bugs.

But perhaps the most dreaded human-to-cockroach encounter is the legendary ear infestation. Although it sounds too horrible to be anything more than an urban legend, in fact, cases of
German cockroaches crawling into people's ears and getting stuck
there have been well documented in medical literature. Emergency
room doctors can pour oil in the ear to drown cockroaches, but
often have a hard time extracting them afterward. Some doctors
swear by a squirt of lidocaine, which irritates the roach so much
that it can send it running out of the ear and across the room.

Attempts to rid homes of cockroaches often lead to even more
health problems: epidemiologists have noted that an increase in

home pesticide use, and the overall exposure to the chemicals that results from using them in the home, can pose a more serious hazard than the bugs themselves do. Safer roach baits are available, but cleanliness and a well-sealed home are the best defenses. A recent study showed that the "juice" of dead roaches was an effective roach repellent, but this is not likely to catch on as a home remedy.

Meet the Relatives There are roughly four thousand species around the world. *Periplaneta americana,* the American cockroach or Palmetto bug, is a very large roach found throughout the southern United States and along parts of the East Coast.

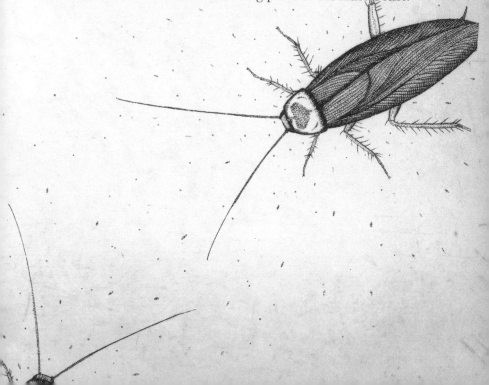

Colorado Potato Beetle

LEPTINOTARSA DECEMLINEATA

Thomas Say, often considered to be the father of American entomology, traveled west as far as the Rocky Mountains in 1820 as part of a military expedition. It was his job to "examine and describe any objects in zoology, and its several branches, that may come under our observation. A classification of all land and water animals, insects, &c. and a particular description of the animal remains found in a concrete state will be required." His team consisted of a botanist, a geologist, an assistant naturalist, and a painter. This was not an easy journey; the group faced severe water shortages, attacks from Indian tribes, illnesses and injuries, and the loss of horses and critical supplies. It is no surprise, then, that when he encountered a small striped beetle feeding on a tough little weed in the nightshade family, he made a record of it but didn't consider it one of the major discoveries of the expedition.

SIZE:
9.5 mm

FAMILY:
Chrysomelidae

HABITAT:
Farms, fields, and meadows where nightshades are abundant

DISTRIBUTION:
North America, Europe, Asia, and the Middle East

The Colorado potato beetle was just one of over a thousand species of beetles Say described in his lifetime—but it didn't earn the name potato beetle until later. By the mid-1800s, shortly after

Say's death, settlers moved into the area Say had explored and began farming there. When the beetles encountered potato crops for the first time, they gradually abandoned the buffalo burr, the wild potato relative they had been feeding upon, and went to work on potatoes instead. To the horror of the settlers, it soon became clear that the beetles could strip a potato plant of all its leaves, decimating a field of the crop. It then set about eating other members of the nightshade family, including tomato, eggplant, and even tobacco leaves.

The Germans believed that Americans were dropping the beetles from planes as a form of aerial agricultural warfare.

It moved rapidly across the United States, from Nebraska to Iowa to Missouri, Illinois, Michigan, and Pennsylvania over a span of only fifteen years. In 1875 a popular science magazine noted that the beetle "has inflicted so much damage, and caused so much alarm in the United States, that the prospect of its succeeding in crossing the Atlantic has raised almost a panic in some European countries."

This was a well-founded fear. European countries banned the importation of American potatoes to keep the beetle out, but by World War I it was impossible to avoid the accidental importation of agricultural pests as American troops marched across the continent. Now the beetle ranges across Europe and through important agricultural areas across much of the rest of the world.

Some have accused Americans of deliberately spreading the pest: A German propaganda poster from World War II depicts red-white-and-blue-striped Colorado potato beetles advancing across a field like soldiers. The Germans believed that Americans were dropping the beetles from planes as a form of aerial agricultural warfare. They coined the term *Amikäfer*—a combination of the German words for "American" and "Beetle"—to describe this enemy insect. One poster reads "Halt Amikäfer," and the other warns that the evil American beetle "threatens to destroy our harvests" and urges citizens to *kampf für den frieden*—fight for our peace.

This bright yellow-and-brown-striped beetle is slightly larger than a ladybug. A female potato beetle lays up to three thousand eggs in her short lifetime, usually producing three generations of beetles in a single season. Those born late in the season can comfortably survive the winter and emerge early the following year to begin the cycle again. Farmers have bombarded the beetles with an astonishing array of pesticides over the past 150 years, only to find that the insects rapidly grow resistant to the chemicals. This is due in part to their prolific reproduction rates; with three thousand offspring, one of them is bound to be born with a mutation that helps it resist a pesticide. Also, the fact that the insects feed off the leaves of nightshades, which are themselves quite toxic, suggests some level of resistance to poisons.

Meet the Relatives   A member of the family commonly known as leaf beetles, which includes cucumber beetles, asparagus beetles, and other dreaded agricultural pests.

THE GARDENER'S DIRTY DOZEN

They may not change the course of civilization. They might not spread the plague or send villagers fleeing for the hills. And they've probably never been implicated in a murder—although they do inspire murderous rages. These are just some of the pests that drive gardeners mad.

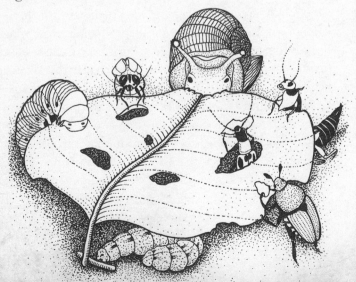

APHIDS

The presence of a few hundred greenish, soft-bodied insects glued to the underside of a leaf, all sucking away at once, is enough to give a gardener nightmares. Over forty-four hundred species have been identified in the Aphidoidea superfamily, many of them specific to a particular plant. Like body lice or ticks, they latch onto their host and start feeding, sometimes transmitting plant diseases in the process. Potato leafroll virus, one of the most serious potato diseases worldwide, is transmitted by an aphid.

But perhaps their most horrifying quality is the way in which aphids reproduce: some species are actually capable of "telescoping generations" in which one female aphid contains within her the beginnings of another youngster, which is herself already pregnant with yet another generation. These parthenogenetic insects require no males to reproduce, and they are capable of carrying on for several generations before mating with a single male.

The oleander aphid, *Aphis nerii,* employs a particularly devious strategy to ensure its survival. It harvests a poisonous substance called cardiac glycosides from the toxic plant and wraps the poison around its eggs to protect them from predators.

Fortunately, a variety of lady beetles, parasitic wasps, and other predatory insects will happily show up and feed on aphids if given the opportunity.

WHITEFLY

Nothing takes the joy out of owning a conservatory more than the whitefly, a despicable pest in the family Aleyrodidae frequently found in greenhouses and on houseplants. (They thrive outdoors as well, but a winter freeze will kill them off.) At only one to three millimeters in length, these tiny winged creatures are so small that they resemble a white powder sprinkled over the leaves.

Like aphids, whiteflies suck plant sap, causing leaves to turn yellow and droop. Some species also transmit disease. Simply brushing by an infested plant will release a cloud of them into the air for a moment, a sight that pains gardeners and greenhouse managers alike. Female whiteflies lay as many as four hundred eggs in their four to six week lifespan. Most greenhouses deploy a species of parasitic wasp—*Encarsia formosa,* which is harmless to humans—to attack them.

SLUGS AND SNAILS

These gastropods require no introduction. Gardeners who must confront them, as they slime their way across the sidewalk and into the vegetable garden, have tried some ghastly and grotesque means of defeating these enemies. From sprinkling salt on their oozing bodies, to setting out shallow bowls of beer to drown them, to picking them off plants by hand and tossing them into the street, everyone has a favored method of confronting the horror. The brown garden snail, *Cornu aspersum,* was introduced to the United States from France in the mid-1800s as an edible delicacy but went on to eat American gardens instead.

Gardeners on the West Coast are fortunate to have an ally in their war against snails: the lancetooth snail, *Haplotrema vancouverense,* is a natural predator of the garden snail. The decollate snail, *Rumina decollata,* has also been introduced from Europe as a predator, but gardeners can rely on a pet-safe iron phosphate bait instead.

CUTWORMS

The larvae of a number of different species of brown or tan moths, mostly in the family Noctuidae, these wormy creatures are usually found underground or hidden beneath fallen leaves, curled into a tight ball. They get their name from their habit of moving along the surface of the soil, cutting down seedlings as they emerge from the ground. Young, vigorous tomato, pepper, and corn plants can be struck down in their prime by a hungry cutworm.

Beetles, spiders, toads, and snakes will eat cutworms—although most gardeners are not desperate enough to release snakes into the garden. Cutworm collars, made from paper cups or plastic tubs and placed around young seedlings to protect them as they grow, are a favorite remedy for gardeners with just a few dozen plants to protect.

EARWIGS

While earwigs may look evil, owing to the nasty pincher-like appendages on their abdomens, these insects from the order Dermaptera aren't really as harmful as most people believe. But they do feed on a wide variety of flowers and vegetables, from dahlias to strawberries. Anyone who has ever been confronted by an earwig while peeling apart a freshly picked artichoke knows what a nasty surprise they can be. Earwigs also dine on aphids and the eggs of other insects, making them something of a do-gooder, too. The easiest way to evict them is to set up traps of rolled newspaper or cardboard tubes, which can be emptied into soapy water in the morning.

JAPANESE BEETLES

Introduced by accident in a New Jersey nursery in 1916, *Popillia japonica* is feared and loathed in the eastern United States. The bronze and green iridescent beetles feed on about three hundred different plants, working collectively to devour them from the top down. Leaves are often left with nothing but the veins, resulting in a lacy pattern that would be elegant if it weren't so destructive. The larvae destroy grass by chewing through the roots, making them a pest of parks, lawns, and golf courses. Americans spend $460 million per year trying to control Japanese beetles and repair the damage they inflict. This process can be difficult and frustrating, usually requiring some combination of picking them off by hand, releasing predatory insects, setting up traps, and replacing plants with varieties that these voracious pests don't eat.

One plant is fighting back: scientists at the U.S. Department of Agriculture have discovered that geraniums (*Pelargonium zonale*) produce a substance that paralyzes the beetles for up to twenty-four hours—enough time for a predator to attack.

CUCUMBER BEETLE

Don't be fooled by these cute spotted and striped beetles. They may resemble yellow or green versions of ladybugs, but they are nowhere near as well loved. The spotted cucumber beetle, a member of the *Diabrotica* genus, and the striped cucumber beetle of the genus *Acalymma,* dine on squash, melons, cucumbers, corn, and other kitchen garden favorites, sometimes transmitting diseases that bring on bacterial wilt and cucumber mosaic virus. Some gardeners cover their young crops with floating row covers to keep them away.

TOMATO HORNWORM

Confronting a four-inch-long-green caterpillar can be a daunting task. These caterpillars (*Manduca quinquemaculata,* the tomato hornworm, and *Manduca sexta,* the tobacco hornworm) can decimate most plants in the nightshade family—including tomatoes, eggplant, and to-bacco—during the month or so they spend as caterpillars. Once they pupate, they emerge as surprisingly large, beautiful sphinx moths that resemble hummingbirds.

As adults they feed on flower nectar, and the sight of them visiting evening-blooming flowers can be quite enchanting. (The caterpillars of some sphinx moths feed on trees and shrubs, not tomatoes, so the presence of a hummingbird-like moth in the garden does not necessary signal a hornworm infestation in the tomato patch.) Because they are so large and easy to spot, gardeners often handpick the caterpillars—but if they seem to have tiny white cocoons attached to them, they should be left alone. This means parasitic wasps have already come to the rescue.

FLEA BEETLE

These tiny creatures get their name from their habit of jumping when disturbed. Members of the leaf beetle family (Chrysomelidae), they chew tiny "shothole" bites in leaves that resemble scattered gunshot. Some species will also chew pits into beets, melons, and other crops. Most plants will outgrow them, though some farmers use trap crops like radishes to lure them away, or they suck them up with a bug vacuum.

CODDLING MOTH

The larva of this moth is the proverbial worm in the apple. It chews tunnels into not just apples but also pears, crab apples, peaches, and apricots, making it one of the most despised fruit tree pests. A number of birds and wasps prey upon coddling moth larvae, but this often isn't enough. Backyard orchardists pull off infested fruit early in the season and set traps baited with pheromones, but if any tree in the neighborhood is unprotected, it serves as a perpetual breeding ground for the moth.

One effective but time-consuming method is to staple a bag around each fruit (called "Japanese apple bags" in the trade) to keep the bugs out—but this means putting up with the rather odd sight of a tree covered in bags all summer long.

One of the more satisfying
home remedies is to point a torch at
the tree and set infested areas aflame,
but experts advise against this.

SCALE

These dreadful sucking insects in the superfamily Coccoidea latch onto a tree and surround themselves with a protective waxy covering so that they resemble a tick. Like aphids, they excrete a sweet sticky substance called honeydew, which in turn encourages the growth of black sooty mold. Their protective shells make them impervious to most forms of control, but it can be quite satisfying to scrape them off a branch with a dull knife. Winter sprays of horticultural oils keep them in check, as do some parasitic wasps.

TENT CATERPILLAR

Few sights are more appalling than that of dozens of fuzzy caterpillars massed around a branch, surrounded by their characteristic silky "tent" that resembles a dense spider web. The caterpillars, members of the genus *Malacosoma,* can strip a tree bare in a bad year. (In other years they are hardly seen at all; they tend to go through boom-and-bust cycles.) One of the more satisfying home remedies is to point a torch at the tree and set infested areas aflame, but experts advise against this for safety reasons and on the grounds that the fire does more damage to the tree than the caterpillars would. Instead, the tents can be cut off and crushed or wrapped in a plastic bag and thrown away.

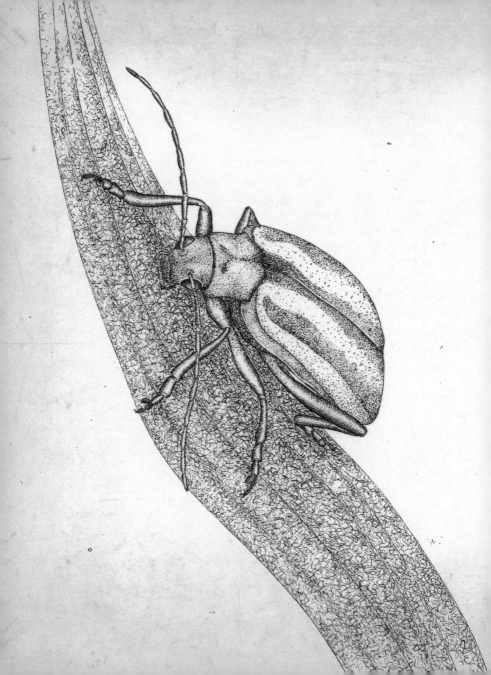

Corn Rootworm

DIABROTICA VIRGIFERA VIRGIFERA *AND* D. BARBERI

Corn faces any number of devastating pests, from the European corn borer to the corn flea beetle to the earworm. They cause billions of dollars in crop loss every year, not to mention the expense and hazards involved with controlling them. But one has proven to be more devious than others at outwitting farmers: the corn rootworm.

Despite its name, the corn rootworm is no worm; it is actually a small beetle not much bigger than a ladybug. During the larval stage, when the creatures live underground and feed on the roots of corn plants, they do resemble tiny white worms—but they emerge in spring as elongated brown or green beetles.

Several species have plagued American farmers for decades, including the western corn rootworm, *Diabrotica virgifera virgifera,* and the northern corn rootworm, *D. barberi.* Both of them probably originated in Mexico and worked their way into what is now the United States as Native Americans began planting corn as a crop. Understanding their life cycle was the first step in fighting them.

SIZE:
6.5 mm

FAMILY:
Chrysomelidae

HABITAT:
Found in close proximity to corn and a few species of wild grasses

DISTRIBUTION:
Mexico, United States, and Europe

In late summer, female rootworms lay eggs underground in the roots of cornstalks. Those eggs hibernate through the winter, and when spring begins to warm the soil, they hatch as tiny larvae that must feed on the roots of a corn plant to survive. Because corn is an annual plant, this survival strategy depends on a farmer seeding in a new crop every year. The larvae continue to feed through the summer, and then pupate in the soil, emerging as full-grown beetles just as the corn is starting to ripen on the stalk. The adults eat corn pollen and silks, then mate and lay eggs underground before they die.

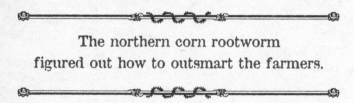

The northern corn rootworm
figured out how to outsmart the farmers.

For a while, farmers used pesticides to kill the insects, but they eventually grew resistant to the chemicals. Crop rotation proved to be the best strategy for breaking the rootworm's life cycle. Because the larvae could not eat any plant other than corn, rotating corn with soybeans would stop them in their tracks. With only the roots of soybeans to eat, the larvae would die off without ever maturing or mating. That would make it safe to plant corn in the field the following year.

This method worked well for decades, allowing farmers to use fewer pesticides and improve the health of the soil. But in the eighties and nineties, everything changed.

The northern corn rootworm figured out how to outsmart the farmers. It evolved to stretch its winter hibernation over two seasons, effectively realizing that the farmer would plant inedible soybeans for a year but would then return with tasty corn in two years. By laying eggs that could remain dormant through an entire year of soybean planting, and then hatch a year later when the corn returned, it was able to outlast the tried-and-true crop rotation and once again become a serious pest of corn farmers. This adaptation is called "extended diapause."

To the amazement of entomologists, the western corn rootworm developed a different way to survive that was just as ingenious as its northern counterpart. Rather than sleep through the soybean rotation, it adapted by laying eggs whose larvae didn't mind eating soybeans. Now that this so-called soybean variant is immune to the practice of crop rotation as well, farmers are once again looking for a solution. New generations of pesticides, as well as genetically modified corn varieties that the rootworms can't eat, may look promising in the short term, but the rootworms have proven that they can outrun such efforts. As one crop scientist said: "It's another magic bullet. We've fired them before . . . in agriculture, problems are not solved forever."

Meet the Relatives Corn rootworms are a type of leaf beetle and are related to the asparagus beetle, the Colorado potato beetle, and a number of other destructive beetles.

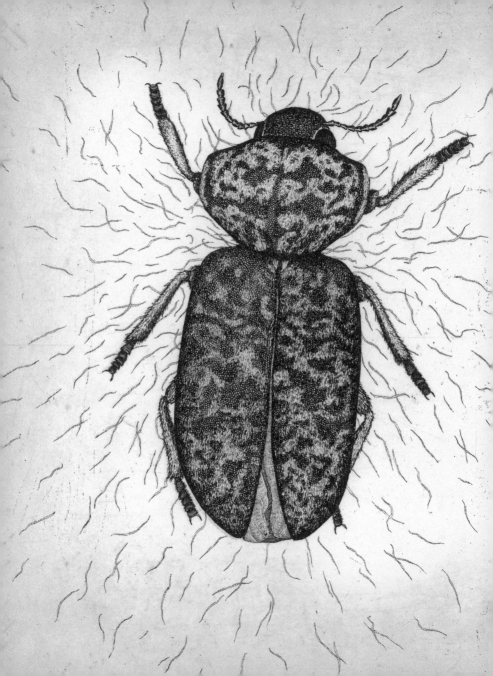

Death-Watch Beetle

XESTOBIUM RUFOVILLOSUM

N ow, I say, there came to my ears a low, dull, quick sound, such as a watch makes when enveloped in cotton. I knew that sound well, too. It was the beating of the old man's heart."

So says the madman who narrates Edgar Allan Poe's frightful story "The Tell-Tale Heart." He describes his victim groaning in the night as he hears the approach of death. And what was the sound that kept the old man—and his murderer—awake at night? "He was still sitting up in the bed listening; just as I have done, night after night, hearkening to the death watches in the wall."

The death-watch beetle to which Poe referred is a bug that sits in the rafters of old homes, quietly munching away at the beams and calling to its mate with the soft tick-tick sound it makes by tapping its head against the wood.

Francis Grose, in his 1790 book *A Provincial Glossary; with a Collection of Local Proverbs, and Popular Superstitions,* included the beetle in his list of "Omens Portending Death." The list begins with such omens as the howling of a

SIZE:
7 mm

FAMILY:
Anobiidae

HABITAT:
Decaying wood in forests, or the timbers of old buildings

DISTRIBUTION:
This particular species is found England; its relatives are scattered across Europe, North America, and Australia.

dog, a lump of coal in the shape of a coffin, and a child who does not cry when sprinkled in baptismal water. The beetle was another sign that the end was near: "The ticking of a death-watch is an omen of the death of someone in the house wherein it is heard."

"Next the ghastly ticking of a deathwatch in the wall at the bed's head made Tom shudder—it meant that somebody's days were numbered."

This old superstition persisted. Consider Tom Sawyer's long night waiting for Huck Finn to come and take him to the graveyard: "By and by, out of the stillness, little, scarcely perceptible noises began to emphasize themselves. The ticking of the clock began to bring itself into notice. Old beams began to crack mysteriously. The stairs creaked faintly. Evidently spirits were abroad. A measured, muffled snore issued from Aunt Polly's chamber. And now the tiresome chirping of a cricket that no human ingenuity could locate, began. Next the ghastly ticking of a deathwatch in the wall at the bed's head made Tom shudder—it meant that somebody's days were numbered."

The larvae in particular are voracious consumers of old, damp buildings; in fact, Oxford's famous Bodleian Library recently required a new roof in order to save its decorated ceiling from the destruction brought down upon it by the appetite of these creatures. Many a homeowner has found the rafters turned to powder after decades of quiet chewing by this destructive pest.

But the beetle's morbid song is hardly its worst quality. These dull, gray-brown beetles bore through moist wood, creating tiny entry and exit holes packed with the powdery residue they leave behind. They prefer hardwood timbers that have already been colonized by fungus, which explains why magnificent old oak buildings in England hold so much appeal. Death-watch beetles can also be found in books and heavy antique furniture. Under the most advantageous circumstances they may live for five to seven years, undermining homes, cathedrals, and libraries, as well as driving insomniacs crazy.

An entomologist writing for *Harper's* magazine in 1861 may have said it best when she described a trip to visit a friend in the country. "The first night I fancied I should have gone mad before morning," she said. "The walls of the bed-room were papered, and from them beat, as it were, a thousand watches—tick, tick, tick . . . But at last the welcome morning dawned, and early I was down in the library; even here every book, on shelf above shelf, was riotous with tick, tick, tick . . . The house was a huge clock, with thousands of pendulums ticking from morning till night. I was careful not to allow my great discomfort to annoy others. I argued, what they could tolerate, surely I could; and in a few days habit had rendered the fearful, dreaded ticking a positive necessity."

Meet the Relatives The cigarette beetle, *Lasioderma serricorne,* the drugstore beetle, *Stegobium paniceum,* and other pests of furniture, books, and stored food are related to the death-watch beetle.

BOOKWORMS

Through and through th' inspir'd leaves,
Ye maggots, make your windings;
But O respect his lordship's taste,
And spare his golden bindings.

Robert Burns wrote those lines in a poem called "The Bookworms," but in fact, there is no such thing as a worm that eats books. Even in the dampest and moldiest of libraries, the pages of a book would be far too dry to meet the needs of a moist creature like a worm. Instead, the insects most injurious to books tend to be those species of lice, beetles, moths, roaches, and other scavengers that are attracted to the surprisingly nutritious ingredients found on bookshelves.

What a glorious buffet a book can be! Consider all the natural ingredients used to print and bind a book: paper made of cotton, rice, hemp, or pulped wood; covers of animal skin, wood, and silk fabric; bindings of paste and glue and thread. Rare old volumes printed on vellum—a kind of parchment made from animal skin—are particularly tempting to necrophagous, or corpse-eating, insects.

Over the years, various noxious substances have been employed to rid books of bugs, including wood creosote, cedar oil, citrus leaves, hydrocyanic acid gas (a cyanide gas that was used by Nazis in concentration camps), carbolic acid (also used in concentration camps and as an embalming fluid), and mercury chloride, a highly poisonous form of mercury. Today some libraries use a deep freeze method to thoroughly rid their collections of pests without leaving a chemical residue behind.

But the best suggestion comes from Lucian of Samosata, a Greek satirist writing in about 160 AD, who criticized "the ignorant book collector" at length, charging that anyone who amassed books to show off their wealth rather than to read them deserved a plague of bugs: "What else is he doing but buying haunts for mice and lodgings for worms?" Desiderius Erasmus, the fifteenth- and sixteenth-century Dutch humanist, echoed that thought when he wrote that "books, to be saved from the worms, must be used."

BOOK LOUSE

Trogium pulsatorium, others

The creature most often blamed for damage to books is the book louse. Its name is misleading—real lice feed on warm-blooded creatures, not literature—and it does not actually eat paper. Instead, this pale, nearly invisible insect is attracted to the mold and fungus that flourishes in poorly maintained libraries. As it eats, pages do experience some collateral damage, but the real significance of a book lice infestation is the fact that the books have been allowed to mold and rot.

LARDER BEETLE

Dermestes lardarius

This beetle, along with other members of the family known as skin beetles, can be found scavenging corpses for bits of dried skin or raiding pantries in search of ham, bacon, and other smoked meats. In museums they cause serious damage to preserved insect collections, buffalo hides, and taxidermied birds, but some curators have turned the beetles to their advantage. A cousin of the larder beetle called the leather beetle, or *Dermestes vulpinus,* has found gainful employment at museums cleaning carcasses so skeletons can be put on display. One curator at Chicago's Field Museum cheerfully reported that a hungry bunch of leather beetles can strip a dead mouse down to the bone in a matter of hours, while a raccoon corpse might take a week or so. "We give them a free meal and they give us a clean skeleton," he said.

In libraries, these carnivores chew holes in leather bindings and lay eggs inside the spine, or even between the covers of two leather-bound books standing next to each other on the shelf. After about six days the eggs hatch and the larvae tunnel right into the pages of a book to create a safe, quiet haven for their pupation. These tunnels do resemble wormholes, which might explain the origin of the term "bookworm."

SILVERFISH

Lepisma saccharina

The English naturalist Robert Hooke, writing in the seventeenth century, called the silverfish "one of the teeth of Time" for the way it wears at antiquities. He said that this greasy, inch-long wingless insect was "much conversant among books and papers, and is supposed to be that which corrodes and eats holes thro' the leaves and covers." Silverfish actually feed on carbohydrates: the sugars and starches found in everything from glue to paper to fabrics. They also happen to like the taste of shampoos, soaps, and shaving creams, which is why they so often inhabit bathrooms.

DRUGSTORE BEETLE

Stegobium paniceum

Entomologists call this a "cosmopolitan species" because of its wide-ranging and sophisticated preferences—it enjoys books and leather, antique furniture, chocolates, spices, and prescription medications, including opium. A tiny reddish beetle not much larger than a flea, this reviled creature is an enemy of rare book rooms, museums, and pharmacies. It once infested the Huntington Library in Southern California, requiring truckloads of books to be placed into a vacuum fumigator and gassed with a mixture of ethylene oxide and carbon dioxide, killing even its tiny eggs.

BOOK SCORPION

Chelifer cancroides

In about 343 BC Aristotle wrote in his *Historia Animaliun:* "In books also other animalcules are found, some resembling the grubs found in garments, and some resembling tailless scorpions, but very small." He was probably referring to the book scorpion, a strange little arachnid that is not a true scorpion, but does possess a pair of fierce-looking pinchers that resemble those of a scorpion or a lobster. The creature is barely a quarter of an inch long, and while it can be quite alarming to find one between the pages of a book, it actually feeds on book lice, moth larva, beetles, and other insects that pose a far greater threat to literary collections than it does.

FURNITURE BEETLE   *Anobium punctatum*

Any enemy to bookshelves is an enemy to books. This wood-boring beetle does its damage in the larval stage. While these larvae might survive only a season in the outdoors, given a nice, quiet library, they will flourish for two or three years, munching through bookshelves, and taking time to browse bookbindings in search of cardboard or wood boards. Once they've grown fat and strong off some book lover's collection, they'll build a pupal chamber for themselves and emerge six weeks later as a full-grown adult — less than a quarter-inch long, but ready to mate, lay eggs, and continue the cycle. The Jewish National and University Library in Israel discovered the beetles in its collection in 2004, but fortunately their archive of Albert Einstein's letters and papers was spared.

"Books, to be saved from the worms,
must be used."

Deer Tick

IXODES SCAPULARIS

Polly Murray knew that something was seriously wrong with her family. Starting with her first pregnancy in the late 1950s, she suffered from strange, unexplained symptoms: painful body aches and fatigue, bizarre rashes, headaches, joint pain, fevers—a catalog of symptoms so long and perplexing that she took to bringing a list of them to every doctor appointment. Over the years her husband and three children experienced similar problems. At times it seemed like everyone in the house was either on antibiotics, propped up in bed with joint pain, or awaiting yet another round of test results.

The doctors in her hometown of Lyme, Connecticut, never had any answers; her family tested negative for everything from lupus to seasonal allergies. From a clinical standpoint, there was nothing wrong with them. A few doctors recommended psychiatric treatment, and some offered penicillin or aspirin. There was nothing else they could do.

In 1975, everything changed. Armed with the knowledge that a few of her neighbors had similar problems and that several local children had been

SIZE:
2 mm (nymphs are smaller—about the size of a flake of pepper)

FAMILY:
Ixodoidea

HABITAT:
Woods and forests

DISTRIBUTION:
East Coast, found as far south as Florida and as far west as Minnesota, Iowa, and Texas. *Ixodes pacificus* is found in Washington, Oregon, and California, with limited distribution in neighboring states.

diagnosed with an extremely rare juvenile form of rheumatoid arthritis, Murray called an epidemiologist at the state health department. He took down the information but offered no solutions.

A month later, she met a young doctor named Allen Steere. He'd worked briefly at the Centers for Disease Control in Atlanta and was looking for a research project for his postdoctoral fellowship. Connecticut's state epidemiologist had called to tell him about the cluster of juvenile rheumatoid arthritis cases in Lyme. Steere listened to Murray's entire story and began an investigation that led to the discovery of a previously unknown tick-transmitted disease. Although the civic leaders in Murray's hometown were not thrilled by the idea of having a dreadful malady named after their town, the scientists called it Lyme disease, and the name stuck.

Although civic leaders were not thrilled by the idea of having a dreadful malady named after their town, the scientists called it Lyme disease, and the name stuck.

The deer tick, also called the blacklegged tick, lives in heavily populated areas along the East Coast and is responsible for most of the cases of Lyme disease in this country. Its ability to transmit the disease depends in part upon its curious life cycle, which can involve three different hosts as it matures. When the larvae first emerge from eggs in the fall, they feed upon rats, mice, or birds. They overwinter on the forest floor, and in the spring they molt into nymphs and feed again—this time on small rodents or humans. By late summer the nymphs have become adults that feed on large animals, primarily deer, for the last year or so of their lives.

These tick larvae sometimes take the bacteria that causes Lyme disease, a spirochete called *Borrelia burgdorferi,* into their bodies during their first meal. When that happens, they are capable of transmitting the bacteria the next time they feed. In spite of the name "deer tick," the deer themselves don't become infected with Lyme disease. But they do help move the ticks around and bring tick populations into close contact with humans. People who live in tick-infested areas know to watch for the telltale bulls-eye rash, called erythema migrans, that often occurs at the site of an infected tick bite within the first month of infection.

Lyme disease is nothing new. Medical writings dating back as far as 1550 BC referred to "tick fever," and European doctors had been investigating symptoms similar to those caused by Lyme disease throughout the nineteenth century. (In Europe the disease is transmitted by the tick *Ixodes ricinus,* called the castor bean tick for its resemblance to the poisonous seed.) In fact, physicians in Lyme who had been practicing medicine for several decades recalled treating patients in the 1920s and 1930s who had similar symptoms. Today it is the most frequently reported vector-borne illness in the United States, with twenty-five to thirty thousand new infections reported each year.

Meet the Relatives There are roughly nine hundred species of ticks found worldwide.

Filth Fly

MUSCA SORBENS

New Yorkers know Randall's Island as an oasis in the East River dedicated to sporting events, bike trails, and walking paths with breathtaking views of the city. Little League teams play baseball, Olympic athletes train, and rock bands play outdoor concerts in the summer. Accessible from 103rd Street, the island offers convenient sports programs for kids in Harlem and the Bronx.

But the island wasn't always such a desirable place for children to play. It served as a "house of refuge" for juvenile delinquents from 1854 until it was closed in 1935. Children detained there were put to work making hoopskirts, shoes, chair frames, sieves, and rattraps. The girls did cooking, housework, and laundry, and made all the uniforms for the inmates. A half hour to an hour per day was devoted to schooling. Punishments for bad behavior included being sent to bed without supper, a bread-and-water diet, solitary confinement, and beatings. Although the children slept in cells, administrators in 1860 thought it might be

SIZE:
6–8 mm

FAMILY:
Muscidae

HABITAT:
Decaying organic matter, including sewage, garbage, dead animals, and other waste

DISTRIBUTION:
Found in warmer climates worldwide, particularly in areas of human habitation

121

better to house them in hammocks in open rooms, where constant monitoring could prevent "indulgence in solitary vice."

The children did not enjoy this treatment. They responded with outbreaks of violence against the staff and attempts to jump into the East River and swim away. The situation got particularly bad in 1897, when an inspection revealed a sewage system that emitted "offensive odors" and an outbreak of a terrible eye disease called trachoma. Roughly 10 percent of the inmates were infected every year. At the time, the connection between these two problems might not have been clear—but it is now.

Trachoma was once a common illness in the United States. It was frequently seen among immigrants attempting to enter through Ellis Island. It is now almost unheard of in wealthy countries, but is all too common in areas of extreme poverty, refugee camps, and prisons throughout the world.

The bacteria that causes trachoma, *Chlamydia trachomatis,* triggers an inflammation of the upper eyelid, which can lead to a cycle of swelling and scarring that shortens the inner lining, eventually pulling the eyelashes into the eye itself. This incredibly painful condition, called trichiasis, leads to damage to the cornea and vision problems. If left untreated, a person can go blind.

Right now, eighty-four million people are infected with the disease, and eight million are losing their sight. It is found in parts of Central and South America, Africa, the Middle East, Asia, and Australia. While antibiotics can treat the infection, and a corneal transplant can treat vision impairments, these are often not available in poorer countries. The disease is particularly debilitating for women, who cannot cook over a fire or work in the fields with this condition. Thus, women depend on children—usually girls—to stay home and help them rather than go to school. In some cases, women are abandoned by their husbands.

While the disease can be spread through close contact, especially between mother and child, health officials also lay the blame squarely on *Musca sorbens,* a relative to the common housefly that has earned the unflattering name "filth fly" for its habit of swarming around latrines, garbage, and manure piles, then picking up bacteria on its hairy legs and moving it around.

Soldiers in Vietnam reported that the flies were so thick in the mess halls that it was impossible not to eat a few of them with their meals.

Basic sanitation, such as hand-washing and the use of clean cloths to wash children's faces, can check the spread of the disease, but eliminating the ubiquitous filth fly is a bigger battle. In areas with open latrines and garbage piles, the flies are so thick that people quickly give up on swatting them away and spend their days with flies climbing in and out of their noses, mouths, and eyes. Soldiers in Vietnam reported that the flies were so thick in the mess halls that it was impossible not to eat a few of them with their meals.

The solution lies in the construction of latrines designed to keep flies out. One design, called a ventilated improved pit latrine, or VIP, is seen by public health organizations as one of the best approaches to keeping the filth fly out of people's lives. It features a vent pipe covered with a screen to keep flies out. The vent also catches wind currents and uses them for circulation, lifting odors away. A representative of Jimmy Carter's foundation, the Carter Center, recently announced that the foundation had hoped to install ten thousand VIPs in Ethiopia, but villagers were so taken with the idea that they installed ninety thousand. Looking back to Carter's childhood, the spokesman said, "They look just like the outhouses people in Georgia were using 50 years ago."

Meet the Relatives This family of flies includes the common housefly, *Musca domestica,* and stable flies.

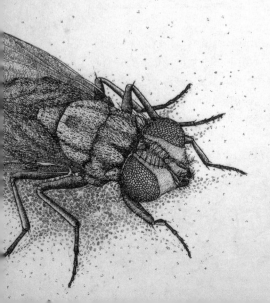

I'VE GOT YOU UNDER MY SKIN

The most dedicated bug-hater can be persuaded to consider the merits of a beetle or a spider, an ant or a centipede. They have their uses, their interesting habits, their own strange and intricate beauty. But nobody loves a maggot. Even the name elicits a shudder of disgust.

These white, wormy creatures are nothing more than baby flies, and no more or less grotesque than any other insect's offspring. They can usually be found clustered around some food source their mother has found for them, and they're doing nothing but eating and growing as children should. What's so offensive about that?

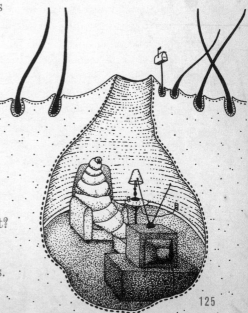

Nothing, except when the thing they are eating is us.

125

HUMAN BOT FLY *Dermatobia hominis*

Travelers returning from Mexico and Central America sometimes come home with more than a great tan. The human bot fly can hitch a ride with tourists, making itself known only when a sore resembling an insect bite doesn't get better.

This fly has an ingenious method of getting under people's skin. It can crawl right into an open wound, but an even more effective strategy is to capture a mosquito, lay eggs on the mosquito, and let it go off in search of a warm-blooded human. The eggs may simply fall off the mosquito when it lands on an arm or a leg, or they may hatch at the moment the mosquito makes contact, enlivened by the warmth of the human host. As the eggs hatch, the larvae crawl right off the mosquito and into the wound it has created. And if there is no mosquito available, a bot fly will happily use a tick for transportation, instead.

If left undisturbed, the larvae will settle under the skin and feed for two to three months before emerging on their own to drop to the ground and pupate. But most people, when confronted with a wound that never quite heals and the uncomfortable feeling that something is moving around under the skin, will not leave it undisturbed. The wound can be painful and itchy, it can ooze a foul-smelling liquid, and some people even claim they can hear the creature moving around. The only consolation is that these wounds rarely become infected, thanks to an antibacterial secretion from the larva itself.

Extraction of a bot fly larva is not always easy, depending on the location of the bite and the overall health of the human host. Some people are sent home and told to wait it out, which can be intolerable for all but the most entomologically curious. Some try to smother it by covering the wound with tape, nail polish, or petroleum jelly, hoping to weaken the larva and pull it out more easily. Doctors have used a simple first aid tool called a venom extractor to remove the creature, and a surgical extraction is sometimes possible, as long as the entire larva can be cleanly removed. One home remedy is to leave a piece of raw bacon over the wound on the theory that the maggot will prefer bacon to human flesh and will leave voluntarily for this new food source.

Any creature with a name like hominivorax— "eater of man"—is best avoided.

SCREW-WORM FLY   *Cochliomyia hominivorax*

Any creature with a name like *hominivorax*—"eater of man"—is best avoided. U.S. agricultural officials knew this when, in 1958, they began an extraordinarily sophisticated campaign to eradicate the fly. They exposed male screw-worm flies to radiation, rendering them sterile, then released them throughout the South. Once those sterile males mated with females, the females would, in all probability, die without mating again, which would bring their life cycle to an end.

Thanks to those efforts, the screw-worm fly was entirely eliminated from the United States, with only sporadic outbreaks that have been fairly easy to treat. This is good news for the livestock the flies were attacking—and for humans, as well.

A pregnant female will lay two hundred to three hundred eggs around a wound or at the edges of mucus membranes—in the eyes, ears, nose, mouth, or genitals of humans and other animals, including cattle. Once the eggs hatch and the larvae start feeding, more females are drawn to the site and they, too, lay eggs. The larvae burrow deeply into the wound, earning them the name *screw-worm* for the way they screw themselves into the flesh and enlarge the wound, introducing the risk of infection. The larvae live inside their host for about a week, then drop to the ground to pupate.

A 1952 case from central California illustrates the problem these flies once posed in the United States. A man who was lounging in his backyard kept swatting at a fly buzzing around his head. The fly disappeared momentarily, but then the man felt a strange itch in his nose. When he blew his nose, the fly came out. Over the next few days one side of his face became so swollen that he went to the doctor. The doctor irrigated his nasal passages and washed out twenty-five maggots. It took eleven more days of irrigation to remove all two hundred maggots that resulted from the fly making one brief visit to the inside of the man's nose.

While the so-called New World screw-worm fly is mostly a dim memory in the United States, it is still found in Central and South America. Another species, the Old World screw-worm *Chrysomya bezziana,* is found in Africa, Southeast Asia, India, and the Middle East. Doctors have noticed that an increase in adventure sports and "Amazing Race"–style treks through jungles and deserts have caused a new generation of Americans and Europeans to become reacquainted with the screw-worm fly.

TUMBU FLY   *Cordylobia anthropophaga*

In sub-Saharan Africa, people dread the arrival of the tumbu fly, whose females lay up to three hundred eggs at a time in the sandy soil, preferably soil contaminated with excrement if they can find it. They are also drawn to clean laundry that has been hung out to dry, depositing their eggs there so frequently that the locals—those who can afford it—know to place their clothes in a hot dryer or iron them to kill the eggs.

Once the eggs hatch, the larvae are able to burrow into healthy, unbroken skin, often without their victim noticing or feeling any pain at all. Over the next few days a nasty boil develops which, if left untreated, will itch and hurt and leak a vile fluid made up of a mixture of blood and the bodily waste of the larvae.

The larvae will leave on their own after two weeks if they aren't forcibly removed first. Although the tumbu fly is only found in Africa, cases have turned up elsewhere, presumably because the eggs hitched a ride on a blanket or article of clothing coming from the continent.

SCUTTLE FLY   *Megaselia scalaris*

This fly, which is found worldwide, gets its name from its habit of scuttling around with short, jerky motions. It has also earned the name "coffin fly," as one of many flies that are attracted to dead bodies. Unfortunately, it is found among the living, too.

Scuttle flies are also known for their horrid attraction to the urinary tract. Cases of urogenital myiasis—infestations of eggs and larva in the urinary or genital areas by scuttle flies—have been documented in areas of poor hygiene, particularly when some sort of wound or infection was already present.

In 2004, an Iranian man working in Kuwait was injured when concrete at a building site fell on him. At the hospital he was treated for fractures and lacerations. After two weeks, scuttle fly maggots emerged from his wound while the bandage was being changed. By calculating the age of the larvae, hospital administrators were able to determine that the man had been infected at the hospital, and that the flies would have had to crawl under his bandage to lay their eggs.

CONGO FLOOR MAGGOT
Auchmeromyia senegalensis

People living in huts south of the Sahara are well-advised to stay off the ground. The Congo floor maggot flies like to lay their eggs on the warm, dry floors of huts or in caves and barns where animals are sheltered. When the larvae hatch, they wander around on the floor at night looking for a warm-blooded creature to feed upon. They will bite humans in the night and drink their blood for about twenty minutes at a time, but apart from painful, swollen bites, they don't transmit disease or burrow under the skin. People who sleep on mats are unable to avoid being bitten, but those lucky enough to sleep in a bed are rarely bothered by these night-time bloodsuckers.

Nobody loves a maggot.

Even the name elicits a shudder

of disgust.

Formosan Subterranean Termite

COPTOTERMES FORMOSANUS

Judging from recent news stories," said entomologist Mark Hunter in 2000, "the Formosan termite appears determined to consume the historic French Quarter of New Orleans. These termites destroy creosote-treated utility poles and wharves, the switch boxes of underground traffic lights, underground telephone cables, live trees and shrubs and the seals on high pressure water lines." At that time he predicted that this invasive Asian termite would be the greatest challenge in the war between humans and insects going into the twenty-first century.

Unfortunately, five years later, Hurricane Katrina proved him right. The most devastating natural disaster in U.S. history killed 1,833 people; it also displaced three-quarters of a million more, making it responsible for the largest mass migration since the Dust Bowl. When the damages were finally tallied, they reached

SIZE:
15 mm

FAMILY:
Rhinotermitidae

HABITAT:
Found underground, in trees, or in attics and crawl spaces of wood structures.

DISTRIBUTION:
Taiwan, China, Japan, Hawaii, South Africa, Sri Lanka, southeastern United States

almost $100 billion. And as New Orleans started to rebuild, it became clear that the pest that has plagued this city for decades may have played a role in its destruction. The seams of the floodwalls that were supposed to protect the city were made of sugarcane waste, a treat that Formosan termites cannot resist.

Could any of this have been prevented? Seventeen years before Katrina, the Formosan termite lost its most dedicated foe. Jeffery LaFage, a Louisiana State University AgCenter entomologist, was out for dinner in the French Quarter in 1989 to celebrate the start of his new program to eliminate termites from the Quarter. As he walked through the Quarter with a friend after dinner, a robber approached them both and shot and killed Jeffery. His death set termite control in the area back by years.

The seams of the New Orleans floodwalls were made of sugarcane waste, a treat that Formosan termites cannot resist.

Fellow AgCenter entomologist Gregg Henderson took up the fight. He sounded the alarm about the infestation of termites in the floodwalls five years before Katrina came ashore, then watched in horror as his worst predictions came true. "I remember watching the news as the floodwalls and levees broke," he said. "I started to get that sick feeling, when you know something's wrong." While poor planning and maintenance certainly contributed to their failure, the role of the Formosan termite could not be overlooked. Henderson has since developed a program to lure termites away from the floodwalls, to places where they could be more easily captured and killed, but he's been unable to get officials interested in his ideas.

Formosan termites have been a problem in New Orleans for decades. The creatures seem to have arrived onboard ships returning to port after World War II. New Orleans' damp, tropical climate and abundant supply of old wood-frame buildings offer the perfect breeding ground for the pest. The French Quarter's row houses make it especially easy for the termites to flourish: any efforts at control undertaken in one building would simply encourage the insects to move next door. Before Katrina hit, the city's residents were losing an estimated $300 million per year to termite damage.

A Formosan termite queen can live for up to twenty-five years, enjoying both a steady supply of food delivered by her workers and romantic assignations with the king termite, whose sole job is to mate with her. Every day she lays hundreds—or perhaps thousands—of eggs. When the larvae hatch, they are fed by worker termites and then grow up to be either workers themselves, who eat wood and feed the colony; soldiers, who use specialized defenses to kill attackers; or nymphs that develop into supplemental kings and queens or "alates," winged creatures that are capable of becoming kings and queens of their own colonies. The swarms of alates around lampposts in the French Quarter from late April through June are so dense that they actually dim the lights and send tourists running.

Some pest control experts hoped that Hurricane Katrina

would have one silver lining—a mass drowning of Formosan termites. Unfortunately, the termites were undeterred. The insects build homes for themselves out of digested wood, feces, and spit; these cartons contain intricate networks of tiny chambers and corridors that hold colonies of several million. The cartons kept most colonies safe and dry throughout the hurricane and the flooding that followed. With home and business owners abandoning both their buildings and the careful regimen of pest control they'd been following to limit their spread, the conditions are perfect for the termite to rise again.

Meet the Relatives About twenty-eight hundred species of termites have been identified worldwide.

THE ANTS GO MARCHING

Justin Schmidt, an entomologist who studies venomous stings, created the Schmidt Sting Pain Index to quantify the pain inflicted by ants and other stinging creatures. His surprisingly poetic descriptions give some order to the hierarchy of ant stings as compared to those of bees and wasps:

1.0   **Sweat bee:** Light, ephemeral, almost fruity. A tiny spark has singed a single hair on your arm.

1.2   **Fire ant:** Sharp, sudden, mildly alarming. Like walking across a shag carpet & reaching for the light switch.

1.8   **Bullhorn acacia ant:** A rare, piercing, elevated sort of pain. Someone has fired a staple into your cheek.

2.0   **Bald-faced hornet:** Rich, hearty, slightly crunchy. Similar to getting your hand mashed in a revolving door.

137

2.0   **Yellowjacket:** Hot and smoky, almost irreverent. Imagine W. C. Fields extinguishing a cigar on your tongue.

2.x   **Honey bee and European hornet:** Like a matchhead that flips off and burns on your skin.

3.0   **Red harvester ant:** Bold and unrelenting. Somebody is using a drill to excavate your ingrown toenail.

3.0   **Paper wasp:** Caustic & burning. Distinctly bitter aftertaste. Like spilling a beaker of hydrochloric acid on a paper cut.

4.0   **Tarantula hawk:** Blinding, fierce, shockingly electric. A running hair drier has been dropped into your bubble bath.

4.0+   **Bullet ant:** Pure, intense, brilliant pain. Like fire-walking over flaming charcoal with a 3-inch rusty nail in your heel.

Ants are incredibly useful, acting as shredders to break down organic matter and recycle nutrients back into the soil and serving as a food source for other small creatures in the food chain. They are also a marvel of social organization, maintaining complex colonies with divisions of labor, sophisticated communication, and the remarkable ability to act as a group to carry out their missions. They wage war, maintain farms of fungus, and build intricate nests with chambers for day care centers and other functions important to the community. But the behavior of some ants is not just fascinating—it's terrifying and, in some cases, brilliantly painful.

FIRE ANT
Solenopsis invicta

Also known as the red imported fire ant (RIFA), this South American native forms colonies of up to 250,000 members that feed on aphid secretions, as well as dead animals, worms, and other insects. They can take over the nests of birds and rodents, devour the shoots of crops like soybeans and corn, and even disable farm equipment.

Their ability to tamper with mechanical and electrical systems is particularly vexing. They chew on the insulation around wiring, switches, and controls, resulting in tractors that won't start, electrical circuits that short out, and air conditioners that won't operate. They have disabled traffic lights and even imperiled the now-defunct super-

collider project in central Texas. In all, the damage caused by fire ants in the United States exceeds $2 billion per year.

But most people fear the fire ant for its vicious sting. Roughly a third to a half of all people living in the fire ant's path—an area extending from New Mexico to North Carolina—get bitten every year. When fire ants attack, usually in response to someone accidentally stumbling into a colony, they bite hard to get a good grip, then inject their venom, causing immediate pain at the site of the sting. If the ant isn't knocked off, it will sting a few more times in the same area. These bites raise a red welt with a white pustule in the center.

A severe attack, and the scratching that often follows it, can introduce infection and leave scars. People working on construction or landscaping crews risk getting hundreds of bites at once when they stumble across a colony—sometimes resulting in extreme swelling of an arm or a leg, which can last a month or longer. In 2006, a South Carolina woman died from such an attack while gardening, as a result of the same kind of anaphylactic shock that affects some people after bee stings.

The attempts to control fire ants has been so expensive, time-consuming, and ineffective that biologist E. O. Wilson has called it the "Vietnam of entomology." Chemical sprays only wiped out the competition, making it easier for fire ants to get established. Now authorities in Australia are actually hunting them by helicopter, using heat-sensing equipment to locate the enormous mounds so that pesticides can be injected directly into the ants' homes.

DRIVER ANTS   *Dorylus* sp.

When driver ants are hungry, they hit the road. In leaderless swarms, they stream through villages in central and east Africa, decimating everything in their path. As many as twenty million ants join the swarm,

enough to build tunnels as they go and overpower grasshoppers, worms, beetles, and even larger creatures like snakes and rats. Because these inch-long ants barrel right through villages and homes, people may be forced to move out during the onslaught. This is not always such a bad thing; the ants wipe out cockroaches, scorpions, and other household pests during their march.

In 2009, an archeologist exhuming the bodies of Rwandan gorillas to do research on evolution woke up one morning to find a river of driver ants streaming through the excavation site. "Just so you know," said one of her colleagues, "this day is going to suck." The scientists donned protective gear and tried to stay as far away from the swarm as possible. By the end of the day, the ants had eaten their fill and moved on. When the team returned to the dig, they realized that the driver ants had done them a favor by removing every other bug from the soil, allowing them to retrieve clean, intact skeletons.

BULLET ANT *Paraponera clavata*

The bullet ants gets its name from the fact that its bite feels like a gunshot. Those who have had the misfortune of getting bitten by this inch-long South American ant say that the pain is overpowering for several hours, then subsides over the next few days. Some people are temporarily unable to use the limb that's been stung, and some report nausea, sweating, and shaking after the attack.

British naturalist and television star Steve Backshall deliberately braved the sting of the bullet ant when he was filming a documentary in Brazil. He joined members of the Satere-Mawe tribe in a male initiation ritual that involved being stung continuously by a swarm of ants for ten minutes. The pain left him screaming, crying, and writhing on the ground. Soon he was drooling and nearly unresponsive, thanks to the

powerful neurotoxins in the venom. "If there'd been a machete to hand," he told reporters, "I'd have chopped off my arms to escape the pain."

ARGENTINE ANT *Linepithema humile*

This tiny, dark brown ant species probably slipped into New Orleans in the 1890s onboard a coffee ship coming from Latin America. The mild and damp coastal climate proved so favorable that the ants spread across the Southeast and west to California. Citrus farmers sounded the alarm as early as 1908, but their attempts at controlling this invasive ant proved ineffective. The latest news about the Argentine ant's ability to form supercolonies that span hundreds of miles sounds like something right out of a horror movie.

These three-millimeter long ants are surprisingly aggressive considering their size. They don't sting or bite people, but they have wiped out colonies of native ants that are ten times their size. The loss of those native ants means the disappearance of a food source for creatures higher up the food chain, including California's coastal horned lizard, which has not only lost its favorite food source, but also must face attacks from swarms of Argentine ants.

The attempts to control fire ants has been
so expensive, time-consuming, and ineffective
that biologist E. O. Wilson has called it
the "Vietnam of entomology."

But the Argentine ant's favorite food source is not other ants; it is actually honeydew, the sweet secretions of aphids and scale. To make sure that these pests produce enough honeydew, the ants actually "farm" the aphids and scale, protecting them while they do their damage to rosebushes, citrus trees, and other plants, and even carrying the pests around to make sure they find enough to eat.

The disruption caused by these ants, which can exist by the millions under just one single-family home, is almost impossible to fathom. They have driven other ants, termites, wasps, bees, and even birds from their nests, and caused damage to agricultural crops. They act in an incredibly organized, militaristic fashion, never going to war with one another, always working together to accomplish their mission.

In fact, entomologists now realize that the population of Argentine ants that extends from San Diego into northern California is one giant supercolony of genetically similar ants. A European colony extends all along the Mediterranean coast, and supercolonies in Australia and Japan are also well established. The members of all of these colonies are so closely related, and so unwilling to fight one another, that they can almost be thought of as one global megacolony that acts as a single entity in carrying out its mission.

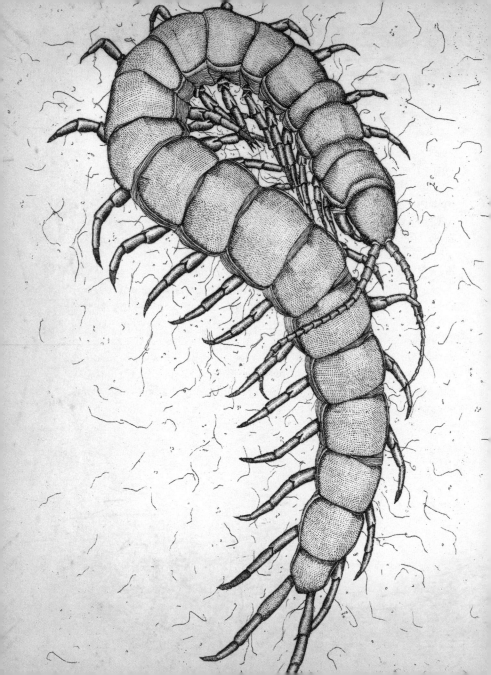

Giant Centipede

SCOLOPENDRA GIGANTEA

In 2005, a thirty-two-year-old psychologist was watching television in his north London home when he heard a strange rustling sound under a stack of papers. He got up, expecting to find a mouse, but instead a nine-inch-long, prehistoric-looking creature with more legs than he could count scuttled away. Fortunately, he had the presence of mind to grab a plastic container and scoop it inside without touching it.

The next morning, he took it to London's Natural History Museum, where an entomologist peered into the bag, expecting to find the sort of run-of-the-mill insect that visitors bring to the museum every day. But when he "produced this beast from his bag I was staggered," the entomologist told reporters. "Not even I expected to be presented with this."

The beast in question was the world's largest centipede, *Scolopendra gigantea*. This enormous South American creature can reach a foot long, and its bite delivers a powerful dose of venom. It may have twenty-one or twenty-three segments; from each segment protrudes one pair

SIZE:
Up to 30 cm

FAMILY:
Scolopendridae

HABITAT:
Moist environments such as the undersides of rocks, leaf litter, and the forest floor

DISTRIBUTION:
South American forests

of legs, with the legs on the first segment being a pair of venom-bearing claws called forcipules. The bite of the giant centipede is powerful enough to cause swelling, pain that radiates up and down the limb where the bite occurred, and even a small amount of necrosis, or dead flesh. Nausea, dizziness, and other such symptoms are not uncommon with a bite as severe as this, but the wounds usually require only simple medical care to treat the symptoms.

The centipedes were hanging from the cave
by their last few legs and catching bats in midair,
demonstrating a rather frightening level
of forethought and ingenuity.

Although people will most likely survive the bite of a giant centipede, small creatures like lizards, frogs, birds, and rats are not so lucky. A team of researchers in Venezuela found one of these giant centipedes hanging upside down from a cave wall, happily munching away on a small bat. After observing the same behavior several times, they realized that the centipedes were hanging from the cave by their last few legs and catching bats in midair as they flew by, demonstrating a rather frightening level of forethought and ingenuity.

In spite of their name, centipedes don't all have a hundred legs. They are distinguished from millipedes in that they have one, not two, pair of legs attached to each segment. The precise number of legs varies by species. And although all centipedes do bite, many are too diminutive to inflict much pain, and some have such small, soft mouthparts that they can't even pierce human skin. (Regardless, centipedes should never be handled with bare hands.) The house centipede *Scutigera coleoptrata,* found throughout North America, might look intimidating, with its fifteen pairs of strangely long legs, but its bite delivers little or no pain. It does eat bed bugs, silverfish, carpet beetles, and cockroaches, so its presence might indicate a more alarming sort of infestation.

Centipedes lack the kind of waxy covering that keep some insects from drying out, so they must stay in moist areas to survive. They breathe through tiny openings behind their legs, and the amount of water they exhale through these openings puts them at even greater risk of dehydration. Their mating practices are surprisingly dispassionate: the males deposit their sperm on the ground where the females can find them. While some males will nudge a female in the direction of the sperm, they otherwise have little romantic contact. The female giant centipede, however, will brood over her eggs until they hatch, even protecting them from predators the way a bird in a nest guards her young.

The pain inflicted by a centipede is mostly related to its size and, as a consequence, the amount of venom it injects. People living in the southwestern United States may rightfully fear the giant redheaded centipede, *Scolopendra heros,* which, at about eight inches long, can deliver a whopping bite. A military physician who has been bitten repeatedly by this species described the pain as a ten, on a scale of one to ten, and reported that over-the-counter medication offered no relief, but that the discomfort and swelling receded completely after a day or two.

And as for the British man who found the giant centipede in his living room? Museum officials originally speculated that it could have hitched a ride from South America to England in a box of imported fruit. Eventually, however, the man's neighbor came forward and confessed that he had purchased the centipede at a

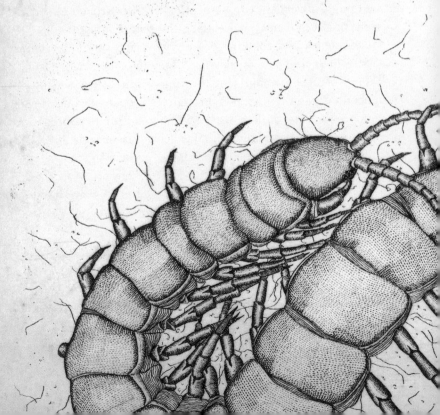

local pet store and intended to keep it as a pet. (They can live for up to ten years, making this a long-term commitment.) The creature was returned to its owner where, it is hoped, it won't be allowed to pay any more visits to the neighbors.

Meet the Relatives There are about twenty-five hundred species of centipedes around the world; the other members of the giant centipede's family are found mostly in the tropics.

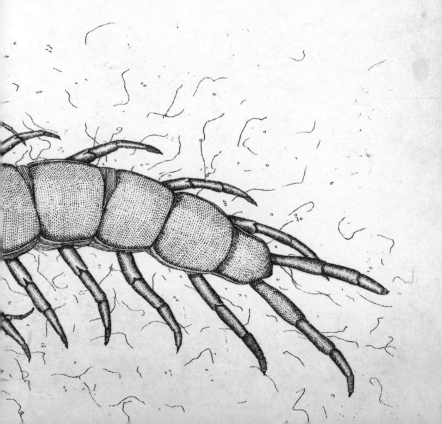

Mediterranean Fruit Fly

CERATITIS CAPITATA

In 1929, a Florida entomologist declared: "The presence of the Mediterranean fly in Florida necessitates a warfare of continental dimensions . . . It is an enemy the United States has never before been compelled to fight. Nothing will be gained by underestimating the seriousness of its ravages, for it works rapidly, silently and persistently, and so far has known no parasitical foe."

And what a war it has been. The Mediterranean fruit fly is so widely feared that when a single fly was found at the Miami International Airport in 1983, it made headlines in the *New York Times*. The fly was even flown to Washington, DC, for a pregnancy test, where, to everyone's relief, it was proven infertile.

The fly had already been in the news a great deal. In 1981, California's governor, Jerry Brown, faced a terrible political quandary: allow aerial spraying of malathion to kill the bug, which would alienate his environmentalist supporters, or refuse to allow it, which could destroy

SIZE:
6.3 mm

FAMILY:
Tephritidae

HABITAT:
Tropical areas and orchards where fruit is plentiful

DISTRIBUTION:
Africa, North and South America, Australia

California's multibillion dollar agricultural industry. He held off spraying as long as he felt he could, but ultimately families in Los Angeles, San Jose, and other areas awoke to the sound of helicopters spraying pesticide over their neighborhoods at night. Those who objected to the spraying were treated to the sight of Brown's director of the California Conservation Corps drinking a glass of diluted malathion at a press conference to prove its safety.

Rumrunners smuggling in bootleg liquor from Bermuda packed their bottles in straw that harbored the flies.

The Mediterranean fruit fly is native to sub-Saharan Africa and probably hitched a ride to the United States on imported produce. (Prohibition may have had something to do with it as well: rumrunners smuggling in bootleg liquor from Bermuda packed their bottles in straw that harbored the flies.) Because every new appearance of the fly in America has been met with strong eradication efforts, it has not yet permanently established itself here.

The fly completes its entire life cycle in just twenty to thirty days. The females deposit their eggs just under the skin of a fruit—often citrus, apples, peaches, or pears—and might fill that hole with several dozen eggs at a time. The eggs hatch and the larvae immediately begin eating the fruit, rendering it useless as a crop. They leave after a week or two—the exact time frame depends upon the fruit's ripeness and the weather—and drop to the ground for a pupal stage that lasts a couple weeks more. The adults emerge, mate, and the females quickly lay a batch of eggs. In good weather, adult fruit flies might live for six more months, nibbling on the crop and laying eggs the whole time. As many as 250 varieties of fruits and vegetables can play host to the flies.

The 1981 spraying campaign kept the fly at bay—for a while. The state spent $100 million to control the pest, only to see it re-occur eight years later. Another round of aerial spraying, coupled with the release of sterile male flies, the installation of traps, and a strict quarantine, averted another disaster. The fly reappeared in 2009, bringing on another round of quarantines and other control measures. Similar efforts have been tried elsewhere in North America, and in South America and Australia, where the pest has threatened crops.

One of the strangest moments in the so-called medfly's history occurred in December 1989, when a group of ecoterrorists who called themselves "the Breeders" sent a letter to the mayor of Los Angeles threatening to release swarms of medflies if they didn't agree to halt aerial spraying of pesticides. In fact, officials did notice unusual patterns of medfly infestation that might have resulted from sabotage. No one was ever caught, and many officials suspected that the threat was merely a hoax.

𝔐eet the 𝔕elatives There are about five thousand species of fruit flies in this family, including *Bactrocera oleae,* the olive fruit fly; *Anastrepha striata,* the guava fruit fly; and *Dacus ciliatus,* the lesser pumpkin fly.

Millipede

TACHYPODOIULUS NIGER, OTHERS

In general, a millipede is not a particularly threatening creature. Unlike centipedes, which actively hunt for prey and inject their victims with venom to subdue them, millipedes creep slowly along the ground, scavenging for dead leaves. They are called "detritivores" for their habit of sifting through the detritus left at the base of plants and breaking it down further to help the cycle of natural composting continue. When attacked, most millipedes do little more than curl into a ball and hope their tough body armor protects them. So what's not to like about these peace-loving vegetarian recyclers?

Their sheer numbers, for one thing. Millipede invasions are not only creepy, they're destructive. Stories of millipedes swarming over railroad tracks have been in the news since the advent of the railroad, but some of the more recent accounts are truly astonishing. Express trains outside Tokyo were brought to a halt in 2000 when the creatures swarmed over the tracks. Their crushed bodies created a wet, squishy mess that made the wheels slip. In Australia the same thing has happened: a nonnative

SIZE:
60 mm

FAMILY:
Julidae

HABITAT:
Leaf litter and forest floor where decaying vegetation is abundant

DISTRIBUTION:
Found throughout Europe, particularly in the United Kingdom, Ireland, and Germany

Portuguese millipede, *Ommatoiulus moreletii,* infested rail lines, forcing the delay or cancellations of trains that simply couldn't gain traction on the slippery tracks.

The situation is even worse in parts of Scotland, where the European black millipede, *Tachypodoiulus niger,* is such a nuisance that residents of three remote villages in the Highlands have been forced to resort to nighttime blackouts to keep the millipedes, which are attracted to light, from creeping into their homes at night and massing around bathrooms and kitchens. A local postmistress told reporters: "They are horrible. They start in April and last year they were still coming in October. It's hard to believe how bad it gets unless you are here and see them."

Monkeys in Venezuela rub the millipedes into their fur and use their secretions to keep mosquitoes away.

A town in Bavaria tried the blackout strategy, but gave up and eventually built a wall around the town to keep millipedes out. The wall, which surrounds the town of Obereichstaett, is made of slick metal with a lip that the creatures can't cross. (Homeowners in Australia have used something similar for years to keep millipedes out of their houses.) One resident of the town said that before the wall went up, he couldn't walk down the street without crushing dozens of them. The smell alone was unbearable.

Millipedes, which can be identified by the fact that they have two pair of legs per segment, do produce a number of unpleasant compounds as a defense mechanism. Some species release hydrogen cyanide, a toxic gas that they formulate in a specialized reaction chamber if attacked. This gas is so strong that other creatures placed in a glass jar with these millipedes will be killed by it. The species *Glomeris marginata* produces a chemical compound similar to Quaaludes, which it uses to sedate the wolf spiders that attack them.

These defensive chemicals are rarely harmful to humans; a person would have to deliberately cover themselves with the secretions of a millipede to experience a rash or burn from them. And, in fact, monkeys in Venezuela search for a four-inch-long millipede called *Orthoporus dorsovittatus* so that they can rub the millipedes into their fur and use their secretions to keep mosquitoes away.

Meet the Relatives There are about ten thousand known species of millipedes, including the giant African millipede, *Archispirostreptus gigas,* which reaches twenty-eight centimeters in length and lives up to ten years in captivity, and the tiny pill millipede, which closely resembles the familiar, but unrelated, crustaceans in the *Armadillidiidae* family that we call sow bugs or roly-poly bugs.

ARROW POISONS

Traditional methods of hunting and warfare sometimes involved extracting insect and spider venoms and applying them to the tips of arrows to make them more deadly. The particular species of insect or spider used has not always been described by observers or revealed by the poisoners themselves, but here, by tribe, are some of their recipes:

SAN BUSHMEN

According to Hendrik Jacob Wikar, a Swedish-born soldier traveling through South Africa in the late 1700s, there was a poisonous worm that could be ground into a powder, mixed with plant juices, and applied to the tips of arrows. Explorers coming after him realized that he was probably referring to the larvae of several species of African leaf beetle, *Diamphidia* sp., whose hemolymph—bug blood—contains a toxin that causes paralysis. The adult beetle resembles a yellow and black ladybug, while the larvae are large, flat, flesh-colored grubs. They are found on one particular small shrub in the *Commiphora* genus native to South Africa and widely used by the San people. Another leaf beetle, *Polyclada flexuosa,* is sometimes used as well.

A carabid or ground beetle, *Lebistina* sp., related to the bombardier beetle, is also used in the poison arrows of San hunters. This beetle is actually a parasite of the African leaf beetle, so they are often found together. The juices of these larvae are sometimes squeezed directly onto the tip of a poisoned arrow and then dried over a fire; they can also be mixed with plant sap or tree gum, which acts like glue to hold the poison on the arrow, or they can be ground into a powder and then mixed with the juices of plants.

Although these poisons can kill a small animal like a rabbit within a few minutes, it takes several days to bring down a large animal like a giraffe, which means that the hunters often spend days tracking the animal and waiting for it to die. But they do work eventually. Thomas R. Fraser, a late-nineteenth-century expert in pharmacology, wrote that these arrow poisons were strong enough to "drive any unfortunate raving mad before he dies in agony."

ALEUT

Native people from Alaska's Aleutian Islands made a mixture of a poisonous plants (aconitum, or monkshood), rotten animal brains and fat, and an unspecified poisonous worm or caterpillar.

HAVASUPAI

These tribespeople, who once lived in and around the Grand Canyon, made use of what was described only as a "small black biting bug," along with scorpions, centipedes, and red ants, to make their arrow poisons.

The Jova tribe in northern Mexico made a similar cocktail of rotten cow livers, rattlesnake venom, centipedes, scorpions, and poisonous plants.

APACHE

One tribal member described an arrow poison recipe that involved hanging up pieces of a cow's stomach until it rotted, then holding wasps against it so that they would be forced to sting the meat. It would then be mashed together with blood and cactus spines and applied to the tips of arrows.

POMO

This California tribe was described as using a mixture of rattlesnake blood, spiders, bees, ants, and scorpions, all crushed together to form a poison that could be applied to arrows and then shot over the homes of enemies as a kind of bad-luck curse.

YAVAPAI

This southwestern tribe had perhaps the most complex recipe for poisoned arrows: A deer liver, stuffed with spiders, tarantulas, and rattlesnakes, would be buried and then a fire would be burned on top of it. It would then be dug up and allowed to rot, before finally being made into a paste. One anthropologist recorded the story of a soldier who experienced one of those arrows firsthand. It took only a few days to kill him. (The use of rotten meat, it should be noted, might have introduced deadly bacteria into the victim's bloodstream, along with the poison.)

These arrow poisons were strong enough to "drive any unfortunate raving mad before he dies in agony."

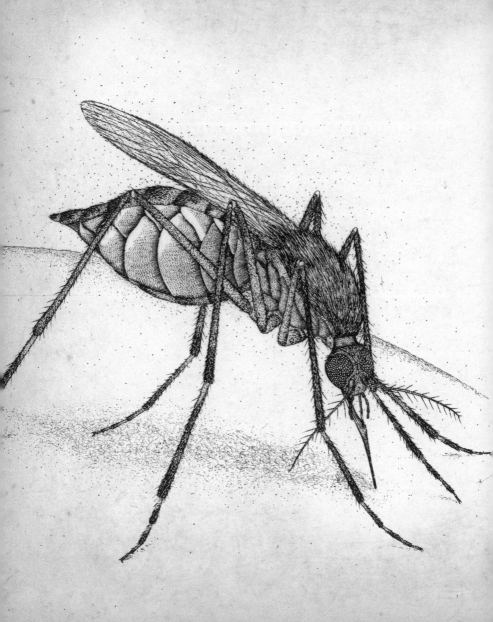

Mosquito

ANOPHELES SP.

O n July 10, 1783, just as the Revolutionary War was coming to an end, George Washington wrote to his nephew that "Mrs. Washington has had three of the Ague & fever & is much with it—the better, having prevented the fit yesterday by a plentiful application of the Bark—she is too indisposed to write to you."

The "Ague & fever" that the future first president of the United States was referring to was malaria, a disease that had plagued him since he was a teenager and also infected his wife. He suffered several bouts of it over the years, along with smallpox, typhoid fever, pneumonia, and influenza. And although the treatment for malaria—quinine, extracted from the bark of the South American cinchona tree—was already in use in Europe, the Washingtons did not have access to it until later in life. Unfortunately, the president took so much of the drug that it caused severe hearing loss during the second year of his term—a known side effect of quinine toxicity.

Malaria has been called our forever enemy because it pre-

SIZE:
Wing length 3 mm

FAMILY:
Culicidae

HABITAT:
Varies widely, but usually found around bodies of water, from lakes to marshes to isolated pools

DISTRIBUTION:
Found in tropical, subtropical, and some temperate climates worldwide

dates humans, as demonstrated by tests on mosquitoes preserved in amber from thirty million years ago. The earliest medical texts made reference to a malarial fever, and some even suggested that an insect bite could be the cause. But the word *malaria,* from the Italian word for "bad air," suggests the commonly held belief that malaria was simply present in the air.

As we now know, mosquitoes are to blame. They transmit not just malaria but dengue fever, yellow fever, Rift Valley fever, and about a hundred other human diseases. Roughly one in five of all insect-transmitted diseases come from mosquitoes, making them the world's most deadly insect. Malaria is believed to have killed more people than all wars combined.

Malaria is caused by a parasite in the genus *Plasmodium*. Female mosquitoes, not males, feed on blood. They must first become infected themselves by feeding on a host and taking up both male and female plasmodia, which then reproduce in the mosquito's body and make their way to the salivary glands. Because mosquitoes live only a few weeks, they may not survive long enough for this to happen. But if it does, and they then feed on someone else, the disease cycle continues. They inject saliva into their victim, where it acts as an anticoagulant. If enough parasites are present in the mosquito's saliva, the victim may become infected—but it is possible to be bitten by an infected mosquito and not get malaria.

Mosquitoes are attracted to their hosts by carbon dioxide, lactic acid, and octenol, components found in human sweat and breath. They also sense heat and humidity around a body. They like dark colors, and they seem to be drawn to people who have been exercising. A French research team recently discovered that mosquitoes are more attracted to beer drinkers. In Rangoon, Myanmar, residents can get as many as eighty thousand bites per year. In northern Canada, when mosquito populations are high, people can get bitten as many as 280 to 300 times per minute. At this rate, it would take only ninety minutes to drain half the blood from a human body.

Today 41 percent of the world's population lives in an area where malaria can be caught. There are nearly five hundred million cases worldwide, and every year over one million people die, most of them young children in sub-Saharan Africa. Experts estimate that controlling malaria worldwide would cost $3 billion. Bed nets play a critical role in protecting people at night when mosquitoes are active, and prophylactic drugs like quinine are also an important strategy in preventing the disease. Currently there is no vaccine.

Malaria did have a brief starring role as a possible treatment for another disease. In 1927 Julius Wagner-Jauregg won the Nobel Prize for coming up with the idea of therapeutic malaria, the practice of deliberately infecting a patient with malaria to cause a fever high enough to kill some infections. He used this technique on late-stage syphilis patients. Once they were cured of syphilis, he administered quinine to treat the malaria. Fortunately, penicillin came along by the 1940s, putting an end to what must have been a miserable way to fight disease.

Meet the Relatives All mosquitoes are found in the family Culicidae. There are roughly 3,000 species, 150 of which live in North America.

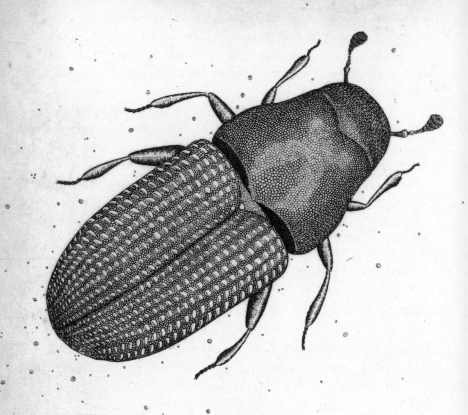

Mountain Pine Beetle

DENDROCTONUS PONDEROSAE

I n an article titled "What the Depredation of Insects Costs Us," the *New York Times* declared that the combined value of everything destroyed by insects would cost us the equivalent of our entire federal budget, and those of several European countries as well. The mountain pine beetle was one of several that "left a trail of ruin" through America's forests by burrowing under the bark, chewing tunnels through the wood, and "leaving millions of dollars' worth of timber in a decaying and useless condition."

When did this alarming news reach the American public? 1907. By the 1930s, a full-scale war was underway in the American West, with Congress appropriating millions of dollars to study and fight the bug that was devouring the forests. But the efforts of Congress were no match for the mountain pine beetle: by the 1980s, the *Times* again reported that the insect was ravaging America's forests, taking out 3.4 million acres in the

SIZE:
3–8 mm

FAMILY:
Curculionidae

HABITAT:
Pine forests

DISTRIBUTION:
Found throughout North America, from New Mexico, Colorado, Wyoming, and Montana, to the West Coast. In Canada, found throughout British Columbia and parts of Alberta.

American West. And 2009 was even worse, with 6.5 million acres destroyed in the United States, and 35 million acres in British Columbia—an area roughly the size of New York state.

The mountain pine beetle, a creature no bigger than a grain of rice, burrows into the bark of a pine tree until it reaches living tissue. There she eats and lays her eggs, sending out a pheromone to other beetles to let them know that she's found a good tree. The tree tries to fight back, excreting a sticky resin that can kill the beetles, but usually that defense isn't enough. As the insects burrow into the tree, they transmit a disease called blue stain fungi that essentially clogs the tree's tissue, making it impossible to transport water up to the leaf canopy.

The larvae spend the winter underneath the bark, keeping themselves warm by turning carbohydrates into glycerol, which acts as a kind of antifreeze to keep them from freezing to death. In the spring, the glycerol is converted back to carbohydrates and serves as an energy source while they pupate under the bark. They emerge as adults in July, mate briefly, and complete the cycle. Mountain pine beetles live for a year, spending all but a few days of that time under the bark of a tree.

In a typical forest, the beetles will start by attacking old, weak, or diseased trees. By going after the older trees first, the beetles actually help "recycle" aged trees and make room for the next generation. But many foresters agree that decades of fire suppression have led to forests with dense populations of older trees, rather than a diverse mix of generations. Now all these older trees are under attack at once. A long, deep freeze might kill off the larvae overwintering under the bark, but recent warmer winters have made it easy for large populations to survive and reproduce.

The devastation brought on by the mountain pine beetle is easy to see from the air. Diseased trees turn red as they die, making what once was a vibrant green pine forest look more like the New England woods in the fall. Unfortunately, there is no good way to control the beetle: natural predators like woodpeckers play a limited role but can't stop an outbreak; chemical controls are cost-prohibitive; and time-consuming treatments like peeling the bark away to expose (and kill) the larvae are not practical on a large scale. Foresters have focused instead on prevention, including thinning trees and allowing some natural fires to encourage an age-diverse forest. The question remains of what to do with the diseased trees. Some experts have suggested turning them into wood chips that can be used to make ethanol or pressing them into pellets that can fuel stoves. In Vancouver, where the beetle has hit hardest, the 2010 Winter Olympics arena featured a roof made from over a million board feet of pine beetle–infested wood.

Meet the Relatives Related to a wide range of other destructive bark beetles and weevils, including the southern pine beetle (*Dendroctonus frontalis*), found throughout Central America and the southern United States, and the European spruce bark beetle (*Ips typographus*), which has devastated spruce forests in central Europe and Scandanavia.

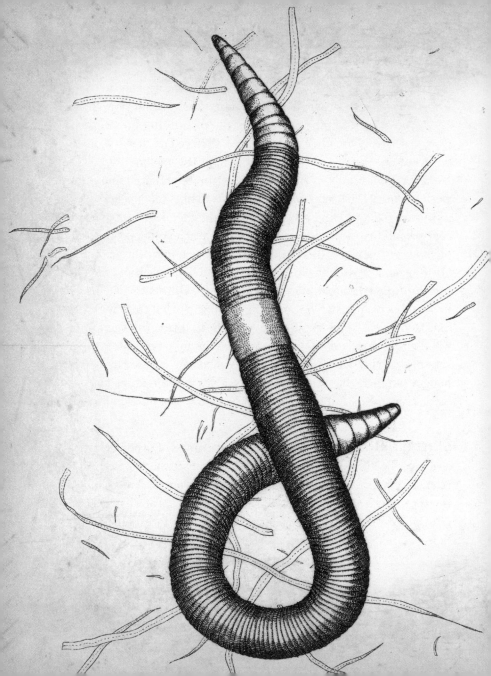

Nightcrawler

LUMBRICUS TERRESTRIS

By the 1990s, scientists at the University of Minnesota had come to expect questions from the public about the strange changes to their forests. Something was happening, people said. The young understory plants—the ferns and wildflowers—were disappearing. There were fewer trees, and almost no young trees. When the snow melted in spring, there was only bare dirt, not the carpet of greenery people expected to see. It was as if the forest had stopped renewing itself. People would call the forestry department looking for answers, but the scientists were just as puzzled.

SIZE:
25 cm

FAMILY:
Lumbricidae

HABITAT:
Rich, moist soils

DISTRIBUTION:
Worldwide

Then one of the researchers, a doctoral student named Cindy Hale, read an article about the forests in New York. "It mentioned, in kind of an offhand way, that increases in earthworm populations might be causing changes in understory plants," she said. "That's when it finally occurred to us to go out into the forest with a shovel and dig."

It would come as no surprise to most people that what they found was earthworms. This shouldn't be cause for alarm—after all, earthworms are good for the soil. They improve drainage, they move nutrients around, they deposit their rich castings around

171

plant roots, and they help break down organic matter. Farmers and gardeners brag about their earthworm populations as indicators of healthy soil. But, as the Minnesota team was about to find out, earthworms are not always as beneficial as people believe them to be. The worms turned out to be a European species. *Lumbricus terrestris,* better known as the nightcrawler, was the largest and easiest to identify. *Lumbricus rubellus,* a smaller species sometimes called a red worm, was also abundant in the soil. In all, they have found fifteen nonnative species living in the forest floor.

Earthworms are not always as beneficial as people believe them to be.

Because Minnesota was covered by glaciers during the last Ice Age, its forests have evolved without any native earthworms. Native North American worms can be found throughout much of the country, but those northernmost portions were absolutely free of worms—until European species arrived.

European worms came to the United States with settlers in potted plants, in soil used as ship's ballast, and embedded in wagon wheels and the hooves of cattle. They moved across the country as quickly as the settlers themselves did. Today the earthworm population in a typical American backyard is likely to be made up mostly of European worms. In most gardens, these worms do only good—but that was not the case in Minnesota.

By monitoring test plots, Hale and her team were able to demonstrate that European worms could completely devour the layer of leaves that fell every autumn. Under normal circumstances, the leaves would remain on the ground year after year, forming a spongy duff layer that native plants required in order to germinate and grow. But rotten leaves are like candy to the nightcrawler. In areas with the heaviest infestation, the duff layer was gone entirely and replaced by a thin blanket of earthworm castings. The native Minnesota trees and wildflowers simply couldn't survive in it.

Solomon's seal, large-flowered bellwort, wild sarsaparilla, and early meadow rue are just some of the plants that are disappearing. Sugar maples, red oaks, and other native trees and shrubs also can't get established in this unfamiliar soil. And as people come into the forests around the Great Lakes, bringing with them live worms for fishing bait, soil for fill dirt, or even tires caked in mud, the earthworms continue to spread. Even building a golf course near a forest can pose a risk, as acres and acres of sod are installed, complete with the earthworms that live in it.

What can be done to stop the invasion of European worms into forests that evolved without them? They can't be evicted; it's not possible to put up a fence to keep earthworms out. Hale and her team found that excluding deer from the forest can make a difference, because the few plants that do manage to survive get eaten by deer. They hope to slow the spread of the worms by discouraging the use of worms as fishing bait and by educating people about the potential hazards of the gardener's best friend.

Meet the Relatives The red worm, *Lumbricus rubellus,* is often found in compost piles, as is the red wiggler, *Eisenia fetida.*

THE ENEMY WITHIN

German physician Friedrich Küchenmeister published a book in 1857 on human parasites in which he described the distress people find themselves in when they discover tapeworms attempting to leave their bodies. "The passage of the segments without feces is a constant annoyance to the patient," he wrote. "The proglottids [tapeworm segments] adhering to the naked body in the trousers, or under the petticoats, being disagreeable, from their clammy coldness, disturb the patients greatly; and women especially are afraid lest the proglottids should fall unperceived upon the ground when they are walking or standing."

But parasitic worms do more than embarrass ladies in petticoats. And often, they are helped along by some other creatures that play a critical role in getting the worms into our bodies in the first place.

PORK TAPEWORM   *Taenia solium*

In the fall of 2008, a thirty-seven-year-old Arizona woman was in for the most frightening day of her life. She was being wheeled into surgery to have a tumor removed from deep inside her brain. It was a risky procedure, but she had little choice: her left arm was numb, she had lost her balance, and she was beginning to have difficulty swallowing. The tumor had to come out.

It must have shocked the medical team gathered around her in the operating room when, in the middle of the procedure, with her skull open and her brain exposed, the surgeon started laughing. He was just so relieved to find out that, rather than an intractable tumor, the woman had been suffering from tapeworms. Removing the worm was a simple affair, and the woman awoke from surgery to the remarkable news that she didn't have a brain tumor after all.

An infestation of pork tapeworm begins when a person eats raw or undercooked pork laden with tapeworm larvae. Inside pigs, the larvae form fluid-filled cysts that don't develop into adults unless they are ingested by humans. Once a person eats pork infested with those cysts, the larvae settle into the intestinal wall, where they mature and reach several meters in length. Adult tapeworms can occupy the intestine for twenty years, releasing thousands of eggs that get discharged from the body through feces. The adult tapeworm may exit the body on its own, or it can be killed with prescription medication.

The Arizona woman was most likely infected not through undercooked pork, but through contact with feces impregnated with tapeworm eggs. One way this could happen is if food handlers infested with tapeworms don't wash their hands after going to the bathroom, allowing tapeworm eggs from feces to remain on their hands when they prepare food. When people swallow the eggs rather than the larvae, a different kind of infestation occurs. The eggs, once swallowed, hatch into larvae that are initially far more mobile, preferring to explore the body rather than remain in the intestine. They can migrate to the lungs, the liver, or the brain.

Although pigs serve as hosts for tapeworms, allowing the eggs to develop into larvae, humans are the only known definitive host. That means that larvae can reach adulthood only in a human.

To the astonishment of the medical community, the talk show host Tyra Banks recently devoted an episode of her show to the so-called tapeworm diet, in which people willingly ingest tapeworm eggs to lose weight. In fact, tapeworms can cause severe digestive problems, anemia, and organ damage, and may actually cause people to gain weight, not lose it, making this a very dangerous diet plan.

Pork tapeworms are estimated to infest one in ten people worldwide, with the rate much higher in impoverished countries. The presence of tapeworms in the brain is now the leading cause of epilepsy worldwide—a tragedy that could easily be prevented with better sanitation.

LYMPHATIC FILARIASIS   *Wuchereria bancrofti* and
                                             Brugia malayi

Also known as elephantiasis, infestation with these parasitic worms causes thick, wrinkled skin and grotesque swelling of arms, legs, breasts, or genitals. Over 120 million people worldwide carry the parasite, with 40 million suffering the most severe symptoms. The parasites require both mosquitoes and humans to complete their life cycle: they can only develop from infants (called microfilariae in this case) to larvae while inside a mosquito, and those larvae can only reach adulthood inside a human. The offspring of the adult worms—the next generation of microfilariae—must find their way back into a mosquito to continue growing and repeat the process.

One bite from an infected mosquito probably won't transmit the disease. It can take hundreds of bites for enough male and female larvae to enter the body, track each other down, and reproduce. Once established, however, the adult worms settle into the lymph system and build nestlike structures that block lymphatic fluid and cause the characteristic swelling. Adults live for five to seven years, mating and producing millions of offspring, which circulate in the blood in the hopes of eventually being extracted through mosquito bites to continue their life cycle.

This disease is found in the poorest parts of the world, including Africa, South America, parts of South Asia, the Pacific, and the Caribbean. Although a blood test can detect the presence of the microfilariae, a strange quirk in their behavior makes this an unreliable method: the tiny creatures only circulate through the bloodstream at night when mosquitoes are biting. During the day, they may not show up on a blood test at all. And treatment is even harder: there is no way to eliminate the adult worms, but an annual deworming pill called Mectizan will kill their offspring and stop further transmission of the disease.

But annual pill distributions are not easy in remote areas or countries torn apart by violence. Now public health officials are trying a new approach: adding the dewormer to table salt, at a cost of only twenty-six cents per bag. In China, the disease was eliminated after the government ordered people to use the salt.

While the idea of distributing medicated salt to the world's poorest people may seem strange or disturbing, it has many benefits. Dewormers kill several other annoying parasites, including roundworms, lice, and scabies. A Centers for Disease Control official working to eradicate lymphatic filariasis called the drug "the poor man's Viagra" because people look and feel so much better without the constant irritation of parasites that they once again find themselves in the mood for love, causing a little baby boom in communities that get the treatment. "I've heard of babies named Mectizan," the health official told a reporter.

SNAIL FEVER   *Schistosoma* sp.

A freshwater snail is to blame for the transmission of this parasitic worm. The eggs of *Schistosoma* worms are excreted from infested people in feces or urine. If that waste goes into a river or lake, the eggs hatch and must then enter the body of a freshwater snail to develop into the next generation. They are then released from the snail, and they wait for a human to wade into the water so they can burrow into the skin and continue their life cycle.

This disease, called bilharzia or schistosomiasis, infects two hundred million people worldwide, primarily in Africa but also in the Middle East, East Asia, South America, and the Caribbean. People develop a rash, flulike symptoms, bloody urine, and damage to the intestines, bladder, liver, and lungs. A single pill called praziquantel, given once a year, treats the disease and prevents further transmission. The drug costs only eighteen cents per pill, and this—along with improved sanitation—may someday eliminate the disease.

ROUNDWORM   *Ascaris lumbricoides*

Ascaris lumbricoides needs no help from a mosquito or a snail to find its way into the human digestive tract. At over a foot long, and roughly the diameter of a pencil, it is perfectly capable of taking care of itself. Roundworms settle into the small intestine, where they live for up to two years. Females can lay up to two hundred thousand eggs per day. Those eggs pass from the body in the stool. Once on the ground, they develop into tiny larvae that may find their way back into the human body. This is more likely to happen in areas with poor sanitation, where children may play on the ground near areas used as a latrine, or in communities that use improperly treated human waste for fertilizer on crops that they then eat without proper washing.

Once back inside the body, the worms spend about two weeks in the lungs, then move into the throat, where they are swallowed so that they can reach the small intestine and grow into an adult. In the worst cases, people can harbor several hundred adult roundworms in their intestines. Oddly, the worms are greatly troubled by general anesthesia, and have been known to flee the body via the nose or mouth on the operating table. In areas where roundworm infestations are common, surgeons have learned to administer deworming medications before surgery to prevent startled roundworms from blocking intubation tubes as they attempt to exit the body.

Although some people experience only mild abdominal symptoms, a serious case of roundworm infestation (called ascariasis) can lead to respiratory problems, nutritional deficiencies, organ damage, and severe allergic reactions. An estimated 1.5 billion people—up to one-quarter of the world's population—are infested with roundworms. Most of those are children. Roundworms kill an estimated sixty thousand people per year, mainly through intestinal blockages. Infestations are found in tropical and subtropical regions around the world and sometimes in southern regions of the United States. Prescription medications can kill the worms and a soil bacterium called Bt (*Bacillus thuringiensis*), which is used to control nematodes in soil, shows promise in treating people as well. But improved sanitation is the only sure way to eliminate the disease.

GUINEA WORM   *Dracunculus medinensis*

President Jimmy Carter saw Guinea worm infestations firsthand in 1988, when he was visiting a village in Ghana as part of the Carter Center's humanitarian work. Over half of the people in the village were debilitated by the worms. He told reporters: "My most vivid memory was of a beautiful young 19-year-old-or-so woman with a worm emerging from her breast. Later we heard that she had eleven more come out that season."

Dracunculiasis, more commonly known as Guinea worm disease, is an ancient affliction that has been found in Egyptian mummies. It is transmitted by a tiny freshwater crustacean called a copepod that people swallow when they drink from ponds or other unclean water sources. Once they swallow it, the copepod dies but the guinea worms inhabiting it move into the small intestine to grow and mate. The male dies, but the female eventually reaches two to three feet in length, resembling a long strand of spaghetti. She burrows into connective tissue, around joints, or alongside the bones of the arms and legs.

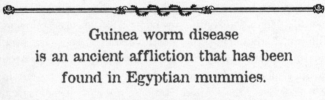

Guinea worm disease
is an ancient affliction that has been
found in Egyptian mummies.

A person might not know they were infested until a year had passed. At that point, the female decides she is ready to leave, and moves near the skin, creating blisters that rupture after a few days. Soaking the wound in cool water brings some relief from the burning pain—which is exactly what the worm is counting on. As soon as her victim drops an arm or leg in the water, she emerges slightly from the skin and releases millions of larvae, thus perpetuating the life cycle. Worst of all, she takes her time exiting the body, and any attempts to grab her or cut her into pieces will only result in the worm retreating back into her hole and emerging later somewhere else.

Treating people is not easy, as there is no medication that works against the worm. Instead, people have to wait for the parasite to show herself, then gingerly wrap a piece of gauze or tie a stick around the bit that emerges from the skin so that she cannot retreat inside again. Every day, inch by inch, the visible part of the worm is wrapped up until, after about a month, she has slithered out entirely.

The fight against Guinea worm disease is remarkable in that it has been so effective. Twenty years ago there were 3.5 million cases in twenty countries throughout Africa and Asia, and now only 3,500 cases remain, primarily in Ghana, the Sudan, and Ethiopia. To stop the disease, people learned to filter their water through mesh cloths or straws that they could carry with them.

If current efforts to fight the parasite continue, Guinea worm disease will become the first parasitic disease to be eliminated completely and the first human disease of any kind to be wiped out without any assistance from vaccines or medications.

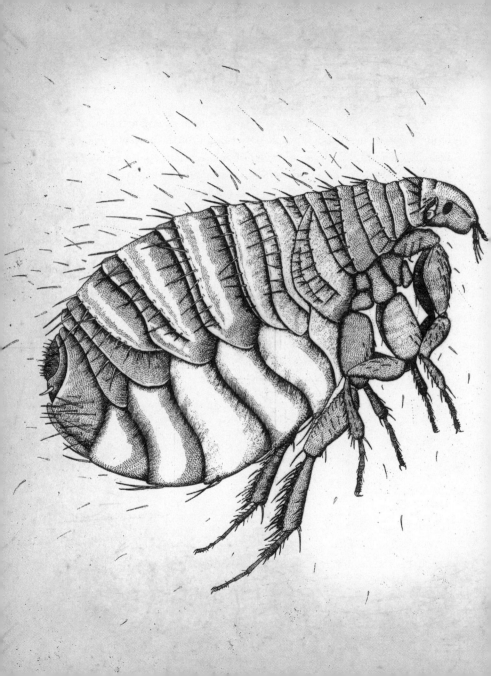

Oriental Rat Flea

XENOPSYLLA CHEOPIS

O n an autumn day in 1907, two boys in San Francisco found a dead rat in the cellar. Inspired by their father, an undertaker, they decided to find a coffin for the rat and give it a proper funeral. This occupied them for one happy afternoon—perhaps the last such carefree day of their youth. When they ran home for dinner that night, they brought along a souvenir of their adventures: bloodthirsty, plague-infested fleas, starved for a meal after their host had died.

The rat flea would prefer to leave humans, cats, dogs, and chickens alone, but when rat populations experience a massive die-off—as they do during epidemics of the plague—the fleas have no choice but to turn to other warm-blooded creatures for their food. This is exactly what happened to those two unfortunate boys. Within a month the plague had claimed their parents but spared the boys, leaving them orphans.

This particular rat had died during an outbreak of the Black Death that began just after the turn of the century when a steamer

SIZE:
Up to 4 mm

FAMILY:
Pulicidae

HABITAT:
Found near rats, their primary food source

DISTRIBUTION:
Worldwide, particularly tropical and subtropical climates, but some temperate zones as well

called the *Australia* left Honolulu and passed through the Golden Gate with its load of passengers, mail, and plague-ridden rats. The rats made their way through the city, which was, at that time, not a particularly clean place: garbage piled up, and makeshift sewers allowed germs and rodents to proliferate. The rats felt right at home. Soon, a few people in Chinatown exhibited the dreaded symptoms: severe fever and chills, headaches and body pain, and telltale red lumps the size of boiled eggs in the armpits and groins. Before long, hemorrhages would give way to enormous black bruises, and death would not be far behind.

The flea's role in this dreaded disease had been discovered in the late 1800s, but the exact mechanism was still a mystery. It was not until 1914 that scientists realized that the gut of the flea held clues as to how it managed to spread the plague so swiftly and efficiently. What they discovered was a remarkable phenomenon called blocking, in which the plague bacteria, *Yersinia pestis,* builds up in the gut of a flea to such an extent that the flea can barely swallow. Instead it is only able to draw the host's blood into the esophagus, where it mingles with live plague bacteria. Unable to swallow because it is so full of plague itself, it regurgitates the blood and the bacteria back into the host's bloodstream. Flea vomit is the true culprit in a plague epidemic.

But that's not all: the fleas are so hungry because of their inability to digest a blood meal that they feed voraciously, moving from host to host in a desperate attempt to fill their bellies. Ultimately the fleas die of starvation and exhaustion, if the plague itself doesn't kill them first.

The Oriental rat flea is just one of over eighty species of fleas that transmit the plague. The disease would have killed many more in San Francisco during the so-called Barbary Plague except for one lucky fact: Oriental rat fleas were in the minority during this outbreak. The species most often found during the San Francisco plague were less prone to blocking and less likely to regurgitate plague bacteria.

Within a month the plague had claimed their parents, but spared the boys, leaving them orphans.

The plague appears to have evolved from a more benign gastrointestinal bug about twenty thousand years ago, and it has run its destructive course through human civilization several times, killing more people than every war combined. An African and European pandemic in the sixth century known as Justinian's Plague killed about forty million people, which represented about a fifth of the world's population at that time. When it reappeared in Europe in the Middle Ages it was called the Black Death. For two centuries it ravaged Europe, killing another one-third to one-half of Europe's population.

Doctors at the time believed that the plague circulated in the air. They ordered patients to keep the windows closed and refrain from bathing, which they believed would expose the skin to the sickening air. Keeping the windows closed wouldn't stop the plague, but it might have stopped the smell. The stench of the dead and the dying must have been overpowering: in large cities like London there was no choice but to pile bodies in thinly covered mass graves. The rat population thrived in such a horrific mess. Ironically, cats were believed to be consorts of witches in those days, so they were killed. Persecution of cats during the Middle Ages nearly eliminated populations of the rat's natural predator, just when Europeans could have used the cats' hunting skills the most.

The plague then moved from China to India to the United States in the early twentieth century. Today, cases of plague still occur from time to time in the American Southwest, but modern antibiotics can usually treat a case that is caught early.

Meet the Relatives The cat flea, *Ctenocephalides felis,* is a relative, as is the dog flea *Ctenocephalides canis*—but in the United States, it is primarily the cat flea that preys on both cats and dogs. They are known to transmit tapeworms.

Flea vomit

is the true culprit

in a plague

epidemic.

Paederus Beetle

PAEDERUS SP.

Heavy El Niño rains brought more than floods to Nairobi in 1998: the wet weather created an explosion of Paederus beetles, also called Nairobi flies for their long association with the region. The beetles creep into schools and homes, attracted to the lights.

They don't bite and they don't sting, so their presence would only be a minor irritant, if not for the fact that when the lights go out, the bugs tend to let go of the lamps and land on whoever might be sitting, or sleeping, below them. The natural tendency is to swat at the bug when it lands, but crushing this beetle releases a surprisingly toxic poison called pederin.

Nothing much happens when the poison first hits the skin. But the next day a rash develops, and a few days after that blisters appear. It takes a couple of weeks for the raw, exposed skin to begin to heal, and during that time people may develop infections if they don't keep the wounds clean. A single beetle can raise a welt the size of a quarter on the skin. A drop of its poison, rubbed into the eye, brings on excruciating pain and temporary blindness, a condition called "Nairobi

SIZE:
6–7 mm

FAMILY:
Staphylinidae

HABITAT:
Damp environments, including woods, meadows, and aquatic areas

DISTRIBUTION:
Found almost worldwide, particularly in India, Southeast Asia, China, Japan, the Middle East, Europe, Africa, and Australia

eye." The problem in Kenya grew so severe that the ministry of health issued warnings urging citizens to keep lights turned off at night, sleep under mosquito nets, and get in the habit of blowing the insects off their skin rather than swatting them. Health officials call this strategy "brush, don't crush."

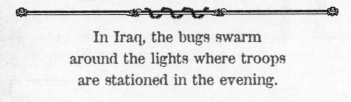

In Iraq, the bugs swarm
around the lights where troops
are stationed in the evening.

Outbreaks of Paederus beetle dermatitis have been a vexing problem on military bases around the world, where bright lights attract the bugs and soldiers might not know to avoid them. In Iraq, the bugs swarm around the lights where troops are stationed in the evening. While bug zappers are widely used on military bases, with the intention of making the area immediately around them a safe place for soldiers to congregate, the Paederus beetles are drawn to the light of the zappers but are not killed by their electrical charge. Soldiers are urged to keep their sleeves rolled down and their uniforms tucked in, a difficult task in the desert heat.

The Paederus beetle is a small, skinny creature with alternating red and black segments and extremely short wing covers that don't resemble wings at all (some species are not even capable of flight). They could easily be mistaken for earwigs or large ants. While the beetles may be annoying in large numbers, they do prey on smaller bugs, including some serious agricultural pests, so farmers generally welcome them in spite of the risks they pose to workers in the field.

There is some speculation that the Paederus beetle is the source of a mysterious legend about a bird that excreted poison droppings. Ctesias, a Greek physician who wrote an account of India in the fifth century BC, described a poison that appeared in the droppings of a tiny orange bird. "Its dung has a peculiar property," he wrote, "for if a quantity of it no bigger than a grain of millet be dissolved into a potion, it would be enough to kill a man by the fall of evening." No trace of this poisonous bird, which he called *dikairon,* has ever been found. Some historians speculate that the actual poison was not a bird dropping, but the bright orange and black Paederus beetle, which sometimes lives in the nests of birds and could be mistaken for droppings. A beetle fitting this description was also known in Chinese medicine as far back as 739 AD as a poison so strong it could remove tattoos, boils, or ringworm. It may have a medical use today as well: the poison, pederin, inhibits cell growth and is under investigation as a possible antitumor agent for use in cancer treatment.

Meet the Relatives There are roughly 620 species of Paederus beetles worldwide. They are a member of the rove beetle family, which includes the devil's coach-horse beetle, *Ocypus olens,* a large European beetle that looks threatening and will bite if provoked, but which is otherwise harmless.

CORPSE-EATERS

The science of forensic entomology—the study of insects to determine the time, location, or circumstances of a death—is not particularly new. A book called *The Washing Away of Wrongs,* written in China in 1235, described how an infestation of flies on a corpse could provide clues in a crime investigation. It even told of a murder that was solved by watching what flies did when the villagers came together and laid out their sickles for inspection. The flies landed on one sickle in particular, perhaps because traces of tissue and blood were present. Confronted with this evidence, the owner of the sickle confessed to having used it to commit the crime.

These methods are still in use today. In 2003, University of California–Davis entomologist Lynn Kimsey received a visit from a police officer and two FBI agents. They wanted to know if she could inspect the bugs smashed against a car's radiator and air filter to determine what states the car had driven through. Their theory was that the suspect, a man named Vincent Brothers, had

driven from Ohio to California to murder his family.
He claimed he never left Ohio. Kimsey agreed to have a
look.

There were thirty different insects on the car, but they
weren't intact: she had to make her identifications from
fragments of wings and legs and smashed bodies. She
found a grasshopper, a wasp, and two other bugs that could
only have been picked up during a drive through the West.
At the 2007 trial she testified for five hours, and the jury
eventually convicted Brothers of murder.

The most common use of forensic entomology is in
establishing the time frame within which a death occurred.

By examining the species of insects that inhabit a corpse, and correlating that with weather data and other information about the crime scene, it is possible to estimate how long a person has been dead, whether the person was wounded before death, and whether the corpse was moved at any point after the crime.

BLOW FLIES

Also called carrion flies, blow flies come from the family Calliphoridae. These blue-green flies are usually the first on the scene after a death, thanks in part to their ability to smell a corpse from over a hundred feet away. They have been known to arrive as quickly as ten minutes after a death occurs, and might lay thousands of eggs in the body. The extent to which those eggs have hatched and moved through their stages of development can help pinpoint the time of a recent death. The answers don't always come quickly, though: sometimes entomologists have to collect the eggs and wait for them to hatch, then count backward to determine the estimated time of death.

Blow flies in the *Calliphora* genus develop quickly from egg to larva to pupa, and that process is accelerated in hot weather, making it important for investigators to know what the temperature has been so that they can correlate that with the size of the creature.

Cocaine also accelerates the maggots' growth. Entomologist M. Lee Goff was called in to clarify an important point of confusion in a murder case in Spokane, Washington. Some of the larvae found on the victim were so large that they appeared to be three weeks old, while others were quite small and would suggest a time of death of only a few days prior. He was able to determine that the larger larvae had been feeding around the victim's nose and that she had been using cocaine shortly before she died. Once the discrepancy in the size of the bugs was cleared up, police were able to rule on a precise time of death.

ROVE BEETLES

Rove beetles in the family Staphylinidae might be among the next insects to appear as the deceased enters a not-quite-as-fresh stage. They are attracted primarily to fly larvae, which means that they tend to show up and devour whatever evidence the first wave of flies have left behind.

BURYING BEETLES

These members of the genus Nicrophorus are attracted to carcasses by their scent and usually turn up to find out if the body is something they are capable of burying. Their reasons have to do with their unique life cycle: when burying beetles find a dead mouse, bird, or other small animal, they actually dig a hole, lining it with fur or feathers they strip from the body, creating a kind of crypt. Often several pairs of beetles will join together in this effort, spending an entire day on the burial process. Once the corpse is completely covered—and therefore protected from other predators—the females lay their eggs inside the crypt so their young will have a food source when they hatch. They even stick around to tend to the brood, making them one of the few insects who actually care for their young.

In the case of a human carcass, the beetles are often found under the body, burying small bits of flesh, possibly tampering with important evidence. They may also lay eggs inside the body since it is too large to bury. There have been cases of the beetles breeding inside stab wounds, for instance. They eat blowfly larvae and sometimes carry tiny mites that feed on blowfly eggs as well, so their arrival on the scene can interfere with the critical information that blowfly eggs and larvae provide.

MITES

These critters arrive in stages as well. The first group are gamasid mites, which ride around on beetles and feed on the eggs of the first wave of flies. Later in the process, tyroglyphid mites, also known as mold mites, show up to feed on mold, fungi, and dry skin.

SKIN BEETLES

In the family Dermestidae, skin beetles are called late-stage scavengers because they often appear a couple of months after death has occurred. These are the beetles used in natural history museums to clean animal skeletons being prepared for display. Another family of beetles may appear later in a corpse's decomposition: the so-called ham beetles in the family Cleridae, which get their name from their habit of infesting dried meats. They have been found in tombs and on Egyptian mummies.

By examining the species of insects
that inhabit a corpse, it is possible
to estimate how long a person
has been dead and whether the corpse
was moved after the crime.

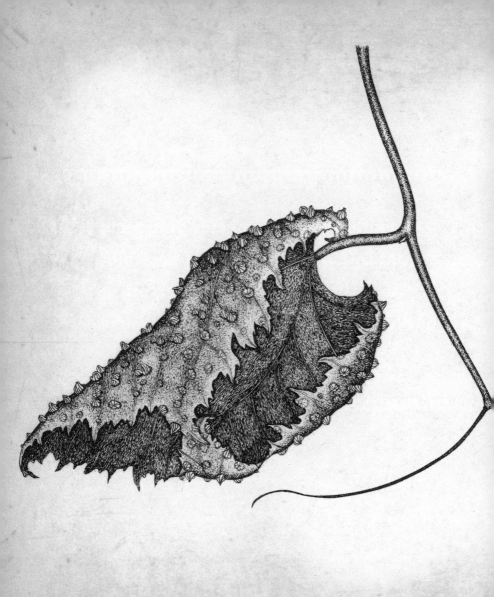

Phylloxera

DAKTULOSPHAIRA VITIFOLIAE

In the mid-1800s, the French wine industry dominated the world market. One in three French citizens made their living from wine. The quality of the vines, the richness of the soil, and the expertise of the winemakers combined to produce wines of extraordinary quality. French physicians recommended drinking wine three times a day, forsaking tea and coffee. People were happy to oblige: the average French citizen was drinking eighty liters, or about one hundred bottles of wine, every year.

And then came the Americans.

Native North American grapevines had failed to produce impressive wines, so Americans took to importing European varieties to help start a domestic wine industry. And French viticulturalists, in turn, planted a few American vines, although they were more a botanical curiosity than a serious crop. These exchanges looked like the beginning of a congenial friendship—until problems started to develop with the vines.

Americans noticed that European vines planted in the United States sometimes failed to thrive. The leaves would turn yellow, dry

SIZE:
1 mm

FAMILY:
Phylloxeridae

HABITAT:
Vineyards

DISTRIBUTION:
Found in various wine-growing regions around the world, including the United States, Europe, Australia, and parts of South America

up, and die. When the dead vines were pulled out of the ground, farmers found no trace of a predator or a disease. Even more alarming was the fact that French vines were starting to succumb to similar maladies. An international search began to find a solution to the problem.

By 1868 French botanists had discovered the culprit: a tiny aphid-like insect they called *Phylloxera vastatrix* (later renamed *Daktulosphaira vitifoliae*). It sucked the sap of living plants and moved on when they died, which explains why it was never found on the dead vines. Later it would become clear that the insect had hitched a ride to France on a native American vine. But for the moment, the only matter that concerned the French was finding a way to kill the insect and restore their industry. First they needed to understand the phylloxera's life cycle.

They discovered that this bug had one of the most bizarre life cycles of any creature they'd ever encountered. It begins when a female phylloxera called a "fundatrix" hatches from an egg and immediately starts to drink from the leaf she was born on. This triggers a hormone in the plant that forms a protective growth called a gall around her. Before long she grows into an adult and—without ever having gone on a single date, much less mated—she lays about five hundred female eggs inside that gall, then dies.

The next generation of females hatch and repeat the process, also forming galls and laying eggs without ever mating. This goes on for months, with perhaps five successive generations hatching, laying astonishing numbers of eggs, and then dying. A single fundatrix female might be responsible for billions of young phylloxera by the time the season is over, sucking the life out of the vines all the while.

The season's last generation falls to the ground and takes up residence in the roots, where a thousand of them might inhabit one ounce of living rootstock. Some hibernate through the winter, and, in the spring, the generation that emerges has wings and is capable of flying to nearby vineyards. Some of these winged creatures lay female eggs, and others lay male eggs. The generation that hatches at that point has only one goal — to make up for the lack of sexual activity on the part of its ancestors. The male doesn't eat — it doesn't even have a mouth or an anus — so it does nothing but mate until death. The females of this generation are capable of laying fundatrix eggs that can begin the whole cycle all over again. At this rate of reproduction, it doesn't take long to bleed the vineyards dry and introduce secondary fungal infections that ensure the end of the grape harvest.

Figuring this out was understandably complicated. But the question of what to do next was even more vexing. Although it was difficult for the French to admit, the only solution was to turn

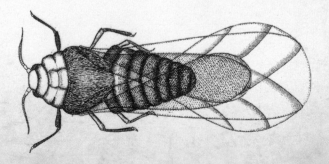

to the very vines that had brought the problem to France in the first place. Native American vines were naturally resistant to this American pest, and grafting fine European vines onto the rough-and-tumble American rootstocks proved to be the only way to save the French wine industry.

But how would the wine taste? French scientist Jules Lichtenstein stated firmly in 1878 that "the vines of France are doomed . . . but the wines of France will live again, reborn on the resistant rootstocks of America." French wines were indeed saved from the phylloxera by the American vines and went on to dominate the world once again. But even today, wines grown on rare pockets of pre-phylloxera vines (including vines in Chile planted by Spaniards centuries ago) are still highly sought after by connoisseurs.

Meet the Relatives Phylloxera are related to a number of other bugs with sucking mouthparts, including aphids, leafhoppers, and cicadas.

The only matter that concerned
the French was finding a way
to kill the insect and
restore their wine industry.

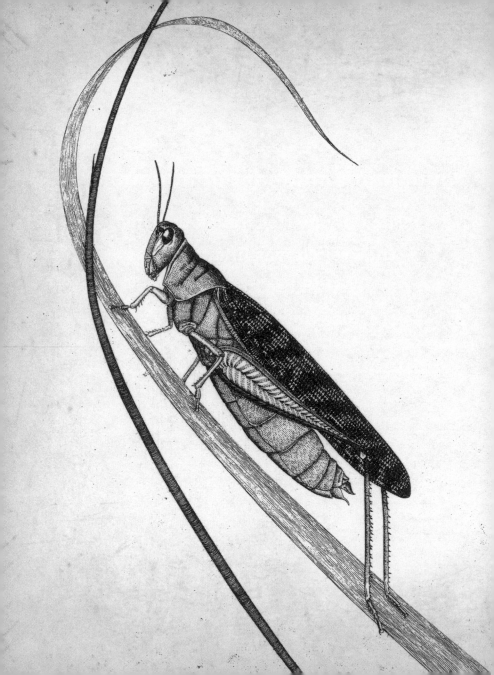

Rocky Mountain Locust

MELANOPLUS SPRETUS

A plague of locusts swept across the American West in the summer of 1875. Farmers watched in horror as a dark shape rose from the horizon and advanced across the sky, moving faster than any thunderstorm or tornado they'd ever seen. The sun dimmed and vanished, the sky filled with a strange buzzing, crackling sound, and then, all at once, the locusts descended.

It happened so quickly that parents had to grab their children and run for shelter. Locusts swarmed over every inch of the cornfields, covered homes and barns, devoured trees and bushes, and even massed indoors so that the floors and walls were thick with them. There seemed to be no end to the assault: millions dropped out of the sky, but millions more moved on to the next county and the one after that.

The sheer volume of locusts that a swarm delivers is almost impossible to grasp. Witnesses reported tree branches breaking

SIZE:
35 mm

FAMILY:
Acrididae

HABITAT:
Meadows and prairies in the American West

DISTRIBUTION:
North America

under the weight of the insects. A layer of insects six inches deep covered the ground. The locusts clogged rivers and their bodies washed into the Great Salt Lake by the ton, creating a putrid wall of brined corpses that reached six feet tall and extended for two miles around the lake.

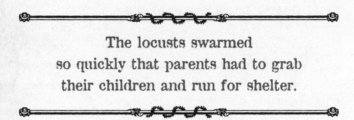

The locusts swarmed
so quickly that parents had to grab
their children and run for shelter.

The size of that ferocious swarm was estimated at 198,000 square miles—larger than the state of California—and it contained about 3.5 trillion locusts. They completely destroyed crops and bred with frightening speed and efficiency: one square inch of soil could hold 150 eggs. Even if only a fraction of them survived, a typical farm could be left with no crops and enough eggs buried in the soil to produce thirty million more locusts. When the larvae hatched in the spring, it looked like the ground was boiling with them.

This pestilence created widespread poverty and starvation across the Great Plains. Some states offered locust bounties to farmers, paying a few dollars for a bushel of eggs or nymphs in an attempt to rid the land of the insects while providing income for its destitute citizens. Some enterprising farmers turned their flocks of chickens and turkeys loose on the swarms, hoping that the free protein source would turn a tragedy into an opportunity. But instead, the birds gorged themselves on the bugs, literally eating themselves to death. The diet of locusts even tainted their flesh, making the birds inedible. Farmers set fires in their fields, doused the soil with kerosene, and resorted to any poison or potion they could get their hands on, but nothing worked. The locusts continued to sweep across the landscape throughout the late 1800s, leaving devastation and mass starvation in their wake.

Little was understood at the time about the life cycle of the Rocky Mountain locust. A locust, entomologists now know, is little more than a grasshopper under pressure. A Russian entomologist named Boris Uvarov, working in the 1920s, proved that certain species of ordinary-looking grasshoppers were capable of undergoing a remarkable transformation during times of stress.

Grasshoppers usually forage alone, spreading out across large areas when food is plentiful. But during a drought, the creatures might be crowded together, and that proximity brings on chemical changes that cause the females to lay very different eggs. The nymphs that hatch from those eggs grow longer wings, have a propensity to live more closely together and travel in dense packs, and are themselves capable of laying eggs that can survive longer periods of dormancy. They even change color. In essence, a fairly benign, stable grasshopper population transforms itself into something entirely different—a migratory plague of locusts capable of swarming and devouring everything in its path.

This explains why the settlers claimed to have never seen

these particular locusts before the ominous swarms arrived, and why plagues of locusts have always been seen as having some divine origin. They are entirely unfamiliar creatures, having transformed themselves from ordinary grasshoppers to larger, darker, never-before-seen invaders.

Even more mysterious, though, was their sudden disappearance. The swarms diminished in size through the turn of the century, and eventually scientists realized that they had vanished all together. The Rocky Mountain locust—the grasshopper known as *Melanoplus spretus*—has not been seen alive since 1902. Although other species of grasshoppers swarmed across the West during the Great Depression, they were not nearly as destructive, nor as widespread, as the Rocky Mountain locust.

Scientists now think that farmers managed to eradicate the locust by doing what they do best—farming. As they turned prairie land into cornfields and cow pastures, they destroyed the insects' only permanent breeding grounds, a series of rich river valleys along the Rocky Mountains where the entire population returned every year to breed. *Melanoplus spretus* now appears to be entirely extinct—much to the relief of American farmers.

Meet the Relatives Not all grasshoppers are capable of turning into locusts. Out of eleven thousand species of grasshoppers, only a dozen or so are known for becoming locusts under pressure.

FEAR NO WEEVILS

Soldiers fighting in the Civil War must have felt that they spent more time battling bugs than the enemy. From the lice that inhabited their clothes, to the mosquitoes that inflicted malaria and yellow fever, to the weevils that bored through their rations, insects were a never-ending problem. While the weevils weren't the most dangerous insects soldiers encountered, they may well have been the mostdemoralizing.

Union soldiers carried a kind of biscuit called hardtack, made of flour, salt, and water.

It was thick, dry, and not particularly tasty, but it resisted mold as long as it didn't get wet—which was difficult under the circumstances. Even if it didn't come out of the package damp and moldy, hardtack was usually infested with weevils. Soldiers developed their own techniques for evicting weevils from their food, such as dunking it in coffee until the bugs floated to the top, then skimming them out with a spoon. But more often than not, bugs were simply part of the meal. One soldier said that "all the fresh meat we had came in the hard bread." He preferred his meat cooked, he said, so he toasted the hardtack first.

Soldiers often joked that they didn't have to carry their rations; the food was so bug-infested that it walked on its own. But behind the jokes were misery and simmering anger. On Galveston Island, in August 1863, the troops staged a mutiny over the lack of wages, the endless drills in the summer heat, and especially the "sour, dirty, weevil-eaten" cornmeal they were expected to eat.

Weevils are small herbivorous insects with elongated, downward-curving snouts. Some have changed the course of history with their destructive behavior.

GRANARY WEEVIL
Sitophilus granarius

Also known as the wheat weevil, it chews into a grain of wheat, deposits an egg there, then seals the hole with a special secretion. The larva lives inside the grain of wheat until adulthood, then it chews its way out to mate and begin the cycle again. This is the species most likely to have turned up in hardtack rations.

RICE WEEVIL
Sitophilus oryzae

In spite of its name, the rice weevil will attack not just rice, but corn, barley, rye, beans, and nuts. Originally from India, it is now found in pantries around the world, particularly in warmer climates. Like the granary weevil, it bores into stored grains to lay its eggs, making it frustratingly difficult to detect. At only two to three millimeters in length, it blends in with the grains it infests.

BOLL WEEVIL
Anthonomus grandis

Perhaps the world's most famous weevil, this small brown creature, no longer than a fingernail, crossed the border from Mexico into the United States in 1892 and quickly went to work devouring the nation's cotton crop. In Georgia alone, cotton production dropped from a peak of 2.8 million bales to just 600,000. In 1922, the boll weevil ate 6.2 million bales of cotton. The Great Depression came along before much progress could be made in getting the insect under control, leading some farmers to simply give up on farming and abandon their land. Other farmers took the opportunity to diversify, planting peanuts or other crops that ultimately proved more profitable—but that changed the South forever. The town of Enterprise, Alabama, even built a monument to the weevil to mark its role in pushing them to abandon cotton in favor of more profitable crops.

Since its arrival, the boll weevil has cost cotton farmers $91 billion, or over $2 million per day. A barrage of poisons were tried on the boll weevil, including a mixture of molasses and arsenic that farmers could brew themselves, a dusting of calcium arsenate, and eventually DDT and other post–World War II insecticides. The weevils developed resistance to those chemicals even before they were banned. Since 1980, the U.S. Department of Agriculture has undertaken a nationwide boll weevil eradication program that involves every acre of cotton planted in the United States—fifteen million acres in all. Using integrated pest management techniques, the weevil has been eliminated from 87 percent of America's cotton fields, and growers have reduced their pesticide use by at least half.

PECAN WEEVIL   *Curculio caryae*

A pest of pecan and hickory trees, this weevil bores into nuts and deposits its eggs there. The larvae eat the inside of the nut as they mature, and people who have the misfortune to crack one of these nuts open will be treated to the sight of a fleshy white grub devouring the kernel.

BLACK VINE WEEVIL   *Otiorhynchus sulcatus*

This enemy of ornamental gardens feeds on plants like wisteria, rhododendron, camellia, and yew. The adults are all females; no males are needed for reproduction. They lay their eggs in the roots of plants, and the larvae devour the roots. The adults feed on the leaves, leaving telltale notches around the edge.

Civil War soldiers often joked that
they didn't have to carry their rations;
the food was so bug-infested that it
walked on its own.

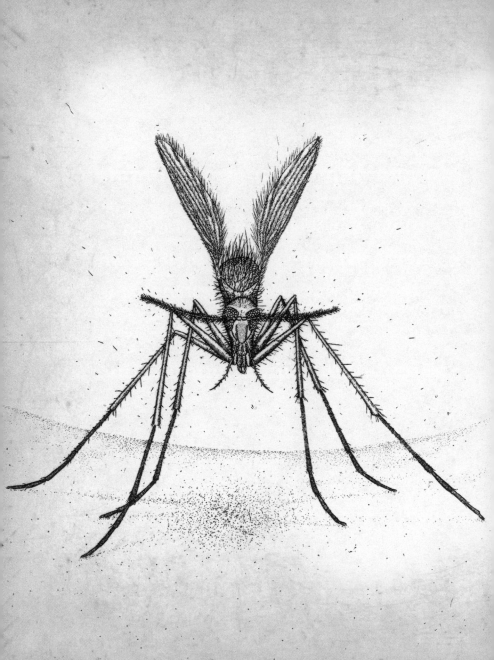

Sand Fly

PHLEBOTOMUS SP.

Britsh television personality Ben Fogle has had plenty of opportunities to be exposed to dreadful exotic diseases. The host of several BBC adventure programs has been marooned on a remote island in the Outer Hebrides, crossed the Atlantic in a rowboat, and raced across the Sahara on foot. He was, it seemed, invincible—until, at the age of thirty-four, he met the sand fly.

This tiny, wheat-colored fly lives for only two weeks as an adult. The females require blood meals in order to nurture their eggs, and while their bites may be almost painless, they can be extremely annoying. In sand fly–infested areas, people often find themselves in the middle of a swarm. This happens because the males, who don't bite, hang around warm-blooded hosts waiting for a female to show up for dinner. So what may feel like an attack is actually an elaborate mating ritual that just happens to have a food source—you—at the center of it. Entomologists call this swarm a mating lek.

When a female bites, she first injects her

SIZE:
Up to 3 mm

FAMILY:
Psychodidae

HABITAT:
Forests, wooded wetlands, and sandy areas near water sources in tropical and subtropical climates

DISTRIBUTION:
Phlebotomus species are found in the Middle East, southern parts of Europe, as well as parts of Asia and Africa. Sand flies in the genus *Lutzomyia*, which also transmit leishmaniasis, are found in many parts of Latin America.

mouthparts into the skin, using her toothed mandibles like scissors so that she can create a pool of blood to drink, and then injects an anticlotting substance that allows her to enjoy her meal a little longer. The flies transmit several diseases, but perhaps the best known is leishmaniasis. This is the disease that nearly killed Ben Fogle after an expedition through Peru.

The sand fly is such a problem in the Middle East that troops stationed there refer to the wounds as "Baghdad boil."

Fogle began to feel some malaria-like symptoms while he was in the jungle—dizziness, headaches, lack of appetite—but he continued filming, then returned to London to train for an expedition to the South Pole. He collapsed during training and was bedridden for weeks while doctors tried to find the answer. Tests for malaria and other, better-known diseases were negative. It wasn't until an ugly sore erupted on his arm that he finally had a clue.

Leishmaniasis is caused by a parasitic protozoa transmitted from other animals to humans via the bite of the sand fly. The disease takes different forms: cutaneous leishmaniasis, which causes a sore that can take months or even a year to heal, and visceral leishmaniasis, a potentially fatal version in which the protozoa infest the internal organs. Another form, mucocutaneous leishmaniasis, causes ulcers and long-lasting damage around the nose and mouth. Fogle had the misfortune to be infected with the more dangerous visceral form of the disease. He required long-term intravenous treatment, but he's now back at work writing, traveling, and filming new shows.

The less harmful cutaneous form of the disease is such a problem in the Middle East that troops stationed there refer to the wounds as "Baghdad boil." In 1991, United States soldiers returning from the Gulf War were asked to not donate blood for two years due to the possibility of transmitting leishmaniasis. There was another outbreak in 2003; although military officials issued warnings about the threat, bug sprays and bed nets were in short supply. It is estimated that over two thousand troops have been infected, but the number could be significantly higher now that troops are treated in the field rather than flown to military hospitals where statistics are kept. Unfortunately, doctors in the United States may not recognize the skin lesions since the disease is not common here—and that could lead to misdiagnoses and delays in treatment for returning soldiers.

Around the world, an estimated 1.5 million people become infected with the cutaneous form of the disease every year, and half a million are diagnosed with the visceral form. The drugs used to treat the disease are themselves quite serious and require close monitoring. Although research on a vaccine is underway, the only way to prevent the disease right now is to avoid the sand fly—which, in spite of its name, is found not just in desert climates, but throughout the tropics and subtropics.

Meet the Relatives There are dozens of species of these bloodsucking flies that transmit disease, but the insect most Americans refer to as a sand fly is actually a more distant relative called a biting midge.

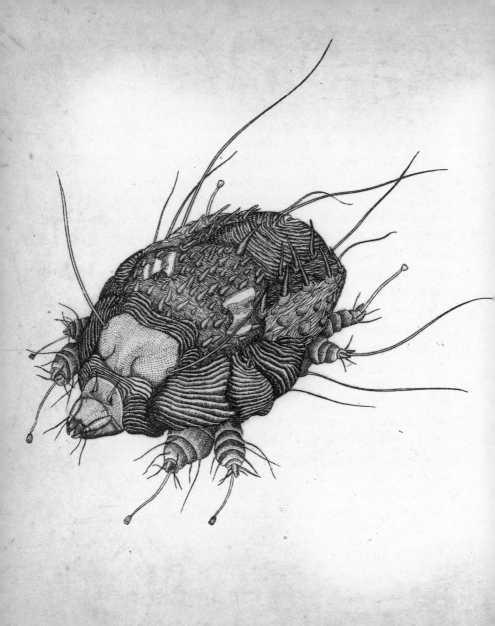

Scabies Mite

SARCOPTES SCABIEI VAR. HOMINIS

Dr. Francesco Carlo Antommarchi served as one of Napoleon Bonaparte's last physicians during his exile to St. Helena. His difficult and demanding patient had suffered from a number of ailments over the years, including digestive problems, liver disease, and a mysterious rash. On October 31, 1819, just a year and a half before Napoleon's death, the doctor recorded this bizarre exchange:

"The Emperor was uneasy and agitated: I advised him to take some calming medicine which I pointed out to him. 'Thanks, Doctor,' said he; 'I have something better than your pharmacy. The moment approaches, I feel when Nature will relieve herself.' In saying this he threw himself upon a chair, and seizing his left thigh, tore it open with a kind of eager delight. His scars opened anew, and the blood gushed out. 'I told you so, Doctor; I am now better. I have my periods of crisis, and when they occur I am saved.'"

Antommarchi was not the first to observe Napoleon tearing apart his own skin. One of his servants wrote that "on several occasions I saw him dig his nails into his thigh so vehemently that the blood came." He was sometimes so covered in blood during military campaigns that his soldiers thought he had been wounded,

SIZE:
Up to 0.45 mm

FAMILY:
Sarcoptidae

HABITAT:
Found on or very near its host

DISTRIBUTION:
Worldwide

when in fact he was just raw from scratching. We may never know exactly what drove Napoleon into such a frenzy, but at least one doctor who treated him diagnosed the rash as scabies.

Napoleon believed it was that moment that he "imbibed the infection ot the itch," from a dead soldier in the battlefield.

Although it was not well understood at the time, the scabies mite certainly afflicted troops during the Napoleonic wars and virtually all wars since. Crowded conditions, the necessity of wearing the same clothing day after day without washing, and mass migrations of poor people during wartime all contribute to the spread of scabies. There were some attempts made during the late 1600s to persuade the medical community that scabies was caused by a parasite, but those ideas were largely ignored. Napoleon's doctors would have most likely believed that scabies was caused by an imbalance of the "humours."

What Napoleon did understand was that scabies was infectious. He described an incident early in his career that begin his long history of skin troubles. During the siege of Toulon in 1793, a gunner was shot while loading a cannon, so Napoleon stepped in and took his place. Both the dead soldier and his equipment were covered in sweat from the excitement of the battle; Napoleon believed that it was at that moment that he "imbibed the infection of the itch, with which the soldier was covered."

By 1865, some decades after Napoleon's death, it was finally understood that scabies was caused by the actions of a nearly invisible mite. An adult female burrows into the skin, usually around the hands and wrists, and lays a few eggs every day. The eggs hatch and the larvae move into an upper layer of the skin, where they form tiny dwellings called molting pouches. They molt into nymphs and then into adult mites, who will mate just once during their short lives, all the while occupying this space under the skin. Once pregnant, the females leave their burrows at last, and walk along their host's body until they find another suitable location to start a new family. In all, a scabies mite lives for one to two months, spending almost all that time under the skin of its host.

People who are infested with scabies might not experience any symptoms at all for the first month or two. Over time, however, they develop a severe reaction to the mites themselves, not to mention the waste products left under the skin. Sometimes a rash spreads all over the abdomen, shoulders, and backside, even when no mites can be found there. Because the mite can live a few days away from its host, it is theoretically possible to transmit scabies through clothing, bedsheets, and toys, although the most common means of transmission is skin-to-skin contact. While Napoleon suffered his whole life from a probable scabies infection, doctors today can treat the condition with a topical cream.

Meet the Relatives A variety of scabies mites infest humans, wild animals, and domesticated animals. The mite *Sarcoptes scabiei canis* causes a type of mange in dogs known as sarcoptic mange.

WHAT'S EATING YOU?

Scabies mites weren't the only parasites to torture Napoleon. General Bonaparte marched into Russia with over half a million men in 1812 and left, defeated, with only a few thousand. What happened? Napoleon himself blamed the cold winter, but scientists now think that it was a tiny, wingless, flattened insect that brought the world's mightiest army to its knees. During their march the soldiers were forced to scrounge food and shelter from peasants in the Polish and Russian countryside, and from those impoverished people they picked up a nasty case of body lice. One soldier wrote that he awoke to a sensation of "unbearable tingling . . . and to my horror discovered that I was covered with vermin!" He jumped up and threw his clothes into the fire, a move he surely came to regret as winter approached and supplies grew scarce.

But it wasn't just "unbearable tingling" that led to
Napoleon's defeat. Body lice carry typhus, trench fever,
and any number of other nasty diseases that can decimate
an army. Napoleon's few surviving
troops were so sick that they had
no choice but to retreat from
Russia, a defeat that marked
the beginning of the end of his
brilliant military career.

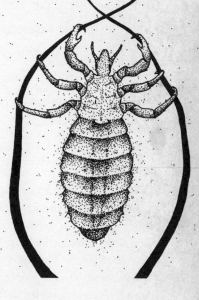

In 1919, at the height of the
Russian Civil War, typhus was
again rampant as a result of the
poverty, crowded conditions, and
warfare that breed body lice,
causing Lenin to say that "Either
socialism will defeat the louse,
or the louse will defeat socialism."

Of the four thousand species of lice around the world,
humans lay claim to only three: body lice, head lice, and
pubic lice. These three species feed exclusively on people,
where they each occupy distinct niches in the ecosystem

of the human body. This fact recently led evolutionary biologists to some startling facts about our history. Head lice date back 7 million years, when humans and chimpanzees shared a common ancestor. Body lice evolved from head lice about 107,000 years ago, around the time humans started wearing clothing. Pubic lice, however, are more closely related to gorilla lice—and were transferred to humans through some sort of intimate physical contact with gorillas, the precise details of which remain a mystery.

BODY LICE   *Pediculus humanus humanus*
                                                    *(*syn. *Pediculus humanus corporis)*

Body lice are, fortunately, unfamiliar to most people. The creatures have evolved to lay eggs in the seams and linings of clothing, not on the body itself. For this reason they're only found among homeless or impoverished people who must wear the same clothes for weeks at a time without washing. The eggs hatch in response to body heat, so clothes that are worn constantly provide the best breeding ground. The newly emerged nymphs migrate to the skin and must feed within a few hours to survive. Over the next week they grow into a full adult and live for a few weeks more, feeding on human blood the whole time. In the most severe cases, up to thirty thousand body lice have been reported on one individual. Even without the possibility of disease transmission, simply being plagued by these tiny bloodsuckers can be dangerous.

Serious infestations cause a strange thickening and discoloration of the skin known as vagabond disease, or pediculosis corporis. People also develop swollen lymph nodes, fever, rash, headache, joint and muscle pain, and allergies, simply from exposure to the lice. Once a person develops high temperatures, the lice will leave them and look for another, less overheated human host, increasing the likelihood of spreading disease.

One of the most common louse-borne diseases is typhus, which is caused by infection with *Rickettsia prowazekii,* a bacteria that also lives in the blood of flying squirrels. The bacteria aren't actually transmitted by the louse's bite. Instead, they are excreted in lice feces, which make their way into the bloodstream when people scratch their bites and inadvertently push the bacteria into the bite wound. Because the bacteria remain viable in lice feces for ninety days, opportunities for infection are plentiful. The disease causes fever, chills, rashes, and eventually delirium, coma, and perhaps death.

About 20 percent of typhus cases are fatal, although death rates are usually much higher during times of war. Survivors used to live with the bacteria in their lymph nodes for years. (Today's modern antiobotics offer a full recovery.) While humans may survive a bout of typhus, the louse never does. The man who developed the typhus vaccine, Hans Zinsser, wrote: "If lice can dread, the nightmare of their lives is the fear of some day of inhabiting an infected . . . human . . . Man is too prone to look on all nature through egocentric eyes. To the louse, we are the dreaded emissaries of death."

In addition to plaguing soldiers living in crowded, unhygienic conditions, the disease also spread to Native Americans after European contact in the 1500s, killing millions. Today outbreaks still occur, primarily in refugee camps, slums, and other areas of mass migrations, severe crowding, and poverty.

Lice were once thought to emerge naturally from the skin, as if born from humans. Aristotle wrote that "lice are generated out of the flesh of animals" and could be seen jumping out of "small eruptions" in the skin. The condition of lice infestation, called "lousy disease" or phthiriasis, was believed to be a punishment for sins. It wasn't until 1882 that L. D. Bulkley put these myths to rest, writing that "all the fabulous stories in regard to lice issuing from abscesses or sores are utterly without scientific foundation—are, indeed, impossibly absurd." A Danish entomologist named Jørgen Christian Schiødte wrote that "the ancient ghost of Phthiriasis could finally be laid to rest among the other dragons and monsters, bred by ignorance."

HEAD LICE *Pediculus humanus capitis*

Because lice have the strange ability to match the color of the skin on which they hatch, an infestation of head lice can be hard to detect—an unpleasant surprise, but not a particularly dangerous one. Head lice do not transmit disease; their presence is not even a sign of uncleanliness. But they are infuriatingly difficult to get rid of and surprisingly common—second only to the common cold in communicable diseases that afflict schoolchildren. An estimated six to twelve million children are infested every year, or about a quarter of all children in the United States. African American children are mostly spared the annoyance of head lice; American lice find it difficult to grip coarse or curly hair, although African lice seem to have no problem with it.

Female head lice lay their eggs along a strand of hair, excreting a little cement to secure them in place. (In fact, a hazard of motherhood for a female louse is the risk of accidentally gluing oneself down as well.) They prefer to deposit their young around the ears or the neck, and this is where they can be most easily seen. Although special medicated shampoos can kill lice, in some parts of the country the lice are growing resistant to those chemicals. A new generation of prescription creams and shampoos are available, but many parents resort to the old-fashioned approach of running a fine comb through wet hair coated in vegetable oil to remove the nits, one at a time.

> Poverty, overcrowded conditions,
> and warfare led Lenin to say,
> "Either socialism will defeat the louse,
> or the louse will defeat socialism."

PUBIC LICE   *Pthirus pubis*

Pubic lice, also known as crabs, lock their claws around a strand of hair and almost never let go. Their habit of feeding in one place for most of their life means that their feces accumulate around them, making for a truly unpleasant situation. They inhabit all parts of the body covered in coarse hair, including eyebrows, chest hair, mustaches, armpits, and, of course, pubic hair. An allergic reaction to their saliva causes unbearable itching, which is usually the first sign of an infestation. They can also infest eyelashes, a condition known as phthiriasis, but they are not known to transmit disease.

Because pubic lice can only survive a few hours off the host, transmission via toilet seats, hotel bedspreads, and other such innocuous means is theoretically possible but unlikely. Sexual contact is really the most efficient means of transmission, which is why the French call pubic lice *papillons d'amour,* or butterflies of love.

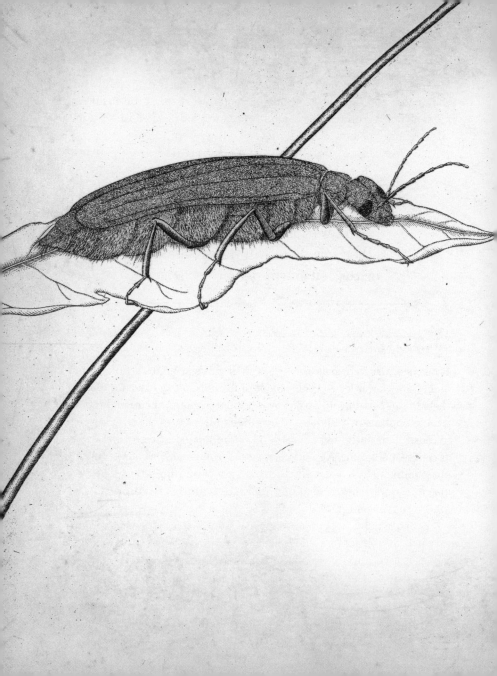

Spanish Fly

LYTTA VESICATORIA

It has been called "the scandal of the poisoned sweets." In June of 1772, Marquis de Sade arrived in Marseilles and sent his valet out in search of prostitutes. The valet was able to convince several women to visit his employer over a single day, hardly an unusual arrangement for Sade. When the women arrived, he offered each of them anise-flavored candies. Some of the women accepted the candy; others refused. (For that matter, some of the women refused to do any number of things Sade proposed, including whipping him with a broom made of twigs.)

Over the next few days the women who had eaten the candy grew seriously ill, vomiting what was described as vile black matter and complaining of unbearable pain. The police got wind of the incident and charged Sade with sodomy and poisoning. He ran off to Italy to avoid imprisonment, but was arrested in December. He escaped in the spring and managed to avoid the law until 1778, when he was arrested again. He would remain in prison for over a decade.

The candy that got Marquis de Sade into so much trouble contained the powdered remains of a beautiful iridescent green

SIZE:
25 mm

FAMILY:
Meloidae

HABITAT:
Meadows, fields, open woodlands, and farms

DISTRIBUTION:
North and South America, Europe, Middle East, Asia

beetle known as Spanish fly, intended as an aphrodisiac. A contemporary of Sade's described the insect's supposed effects: "All who ate them were seized by shameless ardor and lust . . . The most modest of women could not restrain themselves."

The myth of Spanish fly's aphrodisiac powers comes from the defensive chemical it secretes, cantharidin. When ingested, it inflames the urinary tract so much that it can cause a painful and long-lasting erection known as priapism. In sufficient quantities it leads to inflammation of the digestive tract, kidney damage, and even death. Marquis de Sade—and countless others—had confused this condition with sexual arousal and mistakenly believed that it would have a similar effect in women.

The candy that got Marquis de Sade into so much trouble contained the powdered remains of a beautiful iridescent green beetle known as Spanish fly, intended as an aphrodisiac.

The Spanish fly, also known as a blister beetle, uses its poison to repel predators. It also plays a role in reproduction: cantharidin is passed from males to females during mating, and the females use it to protect not just themselves but their eggs as well. In a peculiar way, the poison serves as an aphrodisiac for another species: a fire-colored beetle called *Neopyrochroa flabellata* that doesn't produce any cantharidin itself, but actually takes it from blister beetles and uses it to attract a mate. Females of the species will refuse a suitor who doesn't bring a package of this poison to her so that she can use it to protect her young.

Some blister beetles do manage to get eaten in spite of their chemical defenses. In 1861 and 1893, there were medical reports of French soldiers stationed in North Africa who experienced priapism after eating frog legs. Scientists have long wondered if Spanish fly could have been involved. Cornell entomologist Thomas Eisner cleared up this medical mystery when he fed the beetles to frogs in the laboratory and then demonstrated that cantharidin was found in the frogs' tissues at levels high enough to cause these painful and distressing symptoms. It appeared that the frogs would have to be eaten shortly after they had been feeding on blister beetles, which would explain why eating frog legs for dinner remains a low-risk activity.

The beetles themselves also pose a risk to livestock: some species feed on alfalfa hay, which means that they may inadvertently be fed to horses. Because the larvae eat grasshopper eggs, farmers and ranchers know that a large grasshopper population may mean an increase in blister beetles as well. It would take only a hundred blister beetles to kill a twelve-hundred-pound horse, and even smaller quantities cause colic. Because it is almost impossible to eradicate the beetle, alfalfa fields have to be monitored and mowed according to a specific set of guidelines designed to minimize the likelihood of beetles ending up in the hay.

Meet the Relatives Three thousand species have been identified around the world, with about three hundred found in the United States.

Tarantula

THERAPHOSA BLONDI

C arole Hargis may well be the most inept murderer
California has ever seen. In early 1977 she grew
disenchanted with her marriage to David Hargis,
a Marine Corps drill instructor stationed in San Diego. He had
taken out a life insurance policy on himself, figuring that a military man could face danger
at any time and he should make sure that his
wife (and her children from a previous marriage) would be taken care of. Carole told her
neighbor about the insurance policy and soon
the two women hatched a plan to kill David
and share the proceeds.

The dozen or so murder plots they con-
ceived would be comical if they hadn't ended
so tragically. First, Carole was inspired by an
episode of *Alfred Hitchcock Presents* in which
someone was killed by a hair dryer dropped
in the bathtub. She tried that stunt—except
that David was in the shower, and there wasn't
enough water to shock him. Then she mixed a
powerful dose of LSD into his French toast, which only gave him
a stomachache. Other plans involved bullets in the carburetor, lye

SIZE:
Up to 30 cm, including
legs

FAMILY:
Theraphosidae

HABITAT:
Forests, foothills, and
deserts, primarily in
warm climates

DISTRIBUTION:
North and South
America, Africa,
Asia, Middle East,
Australia, New
Zealand, and Europe

in his martini, sleeping pills in his beer, and a car accident. She hoped to inject an air bubble into a vein while he slept, but the tip of the needle broke, and he awoke in the morning with what looked like a tiny insect bite.

She removed the tarantula's venom sac and hid it in a blackberry pie. Her husband took a few bites of pie but never touched the venom. It was beginning to seem like he was invincible.

And then there was the tarantula pie. Carole kept a pet tarantula and at first she considered putting the hairy spider in bed with him, hoping he would get bitten. But then she had a better idea: she removed the tarantula's venom sac and hid it in a blackberry pie. Mr. Hargis's luck held out a while longer: he took a few bites of pie but never touched the venom. It was beginning to seem like he was invincible.

Eventually, Carole and her neighbor grew desperate and resorted to an old-fashioned bludgeoning, beating him to death in his bed and dumping his body in the desert, where they hoped it would look like an accident. It did not. The police had little trouble discovering the truth, and the women were tried and convicted for their crimes.

Among the many mistakes Carole Hargis made was her misunderstanding of the lethality of a tarantula's venom. Not that they aren't intimidating: the largest tarantula, *Theraphosa blondi,* spans almost a foot in length with its legs outstretched. It spins a trap and waits for its prey to walk by—a mouse, perhaps—then it pounces. With fangs almost an inch in length, it injects its venom and kills the mouse. And like some other tarantulas, it is covered in urticating (stinging) hairs, which it can rear up and fling at an enemy when threatened.

But in spite of this fearful behavior, the bite of a tarantula is really no worse than that of a wasp or a bee. It will certainly sting—in fact, scientists recently discovered that the bite of the West Indian tarantula *Psalmopoeus cambridgei* goes to work on nerve cells with the same mechanism employed by habanero peppers. That fierce, hot pain is hard to bear, but not fatal. For people with severe allergies, the venom can be quite dangerous, but most people will survive it.

In addition to its role in this strange murder case, the tarantula has long been associated with the Italian tarantella dance, which gets faster and faster as it progresses until it is quite frantic. "Tarantism" was a kind of dancing mania found in southern Italy during the fifteenth, sixteenth, and seventeenth centuries that was believed at the time to have been caused by the bite of a tarantula. But in fact, it was more likely caused by ergot poisoning (a fungus that infests rye and contains a precursor to LSD), or it could have been the result of some kind of mass anxiety or hysteria. Regardless, it is highly unlikely that the tarantula is to blame.

Meet the Relatives Over eight hundred species of tarantula are known worldwide.

Tsetse Fly

GLOSSINA SP.

In 1742 a surgeon named John Atkins described a condition he called the "Sleepy Distemper." It afflicted slaves taken from West Africa and seemed to come on with no warning other than a loss of appetite, followed by a state of sleep so deep that not even a beating would awake them. "Their Sleeps are sound," he wrote, "and Sense of Feeling very little; for pulling, drubbing, or whipping, will scarce stir up Sense and Power enough to move; and the moment you cease beating, the Smart is forgot, and down they fall again into a state of Insensibility."

When beatings fail, the doctor advised, one must try anything to awaken them. "The Cure is attempted by whatever rouzes the Spirits; bleeding in the Jugular, quick Purges . . . and sudden Plunges into the Sea, the latter is most effectual when the Distemper is new and the Patient not yet driveling at Mouth and Nose." He had to admit, though, that none of these torturous methods really worked and the disease was usually fatal.

Atkins attributed this strange affliction to everything from

SIZE:
6–14 mm

FAMILY:
Glossinidae

HABITAT:
Found in rain forest, savanna woodlands, and thickets

DISTRIBUTION:
Africa, particularly in the south

"a Super-abundance of Phlegm" to what he saw as the general indolence and inactivity of the slaves, to "the natural Weakness of the Brain." It did not occur to him to investigate the activities of a large, annoying fly that made a *tse-tse* sound as it buzzed around. It would be over one hundred years before the true cause of sleeping sickness was known.

The tsetse fly is found primarily in Africa south of the Saharan desert. Both male and female flies require blood meals to survive. There are about thirty species of the fly, which attack humans on different parts of their bodies. *Glossina morsitans,* for instance, will bite anywhere, while *G. palpalis* prefers to feed above the waist, and *G. tachinoides* generally attacks below the knee. Most tsetse flies are attracted to bright colors; wearing neutral clothing is one way to ward them off.

The flies feed on the blood of wild game, livestock, and humans, sometimes transmitting a protozoa of the genus *Trypanosoma* from one infected creature to the next. The disease moves into the lymphatic system, causing an extreme swelling of the lymph nodes known as Winterbottom's sign. The infection finds its way into the central nervous system and brain, causing irritability, fatigue, aches, personality changes, confusion, and slurred speech. Left untreated, a person may be dead within six months, usually from heart failure.

Although the fly has been around for at least thirty-four million years, the disease it transmits was mentioned only occasionally in early medical writings. It was not until European explorers began moving large expeditions of animals and workers through the African continent that sleeping sickness, called trypanosomiasis, became widespread. In fact, Henry Morton Stanley, the man who found David Livingstone in Africa in 1871, traveled through Uganda with a large party of cattle and men, followed by the tsetse fly, which accompanied the expedition because of the easy food source. He left an epidemic of sleeping sickness in his wake that wiped out as much as two-thirds of the region's population.

There are two forms of the disease, one found in East Africa and another found in West Africa. It is estimated that fifty thousand to seventy thousand people may be infected with the disease today, but that number was ten times as high just a decade ago.

Henry Morton Stanley, the man who found David Livingstone in Africa, left an epidemic of sleeping sickness in his wake that wiped out as much as two-thirds of the region's population.

One strategy for controlling the disease focuses on the tsetse fly itself. Scientists at the International Atomic Energy Agency have found some success with a "sterile insect technique" that involves raising male flies in a laboratory, exposing them to radiation to render them sterile, then releasing them to mate with females, who would then finish their life cycle without actually reproducing.

Unfortunately, the medications available for people infected with sleeping sickness are almost as dangerous as the disease itself. One drug, eflornithine, was originally developed as a cancer treatment and was later found to work against the West African form of sleeping sickness. Because it was so expensive to manufacture, the drug company took it off the shelves in the 1990s, but it started manufacturing it again a few years ago after pressure from the World Health Organization. Recently, a new and more commercially successful use for the drug has helped to spur its production: it is the active ingredient in a new facial cream used by women to treat unwanted facial hair. With a profitable cosmetic use for the drug, it is now once again available to treat sleeping sickness.

Meet the Relatives
There are about twenty-five species of tsetse flies, and they make up the entire Glossinidae family.

ZOMBIES

The insect world has its own version of the Night of the Living Dead. These bugs don't just eat other bugs; they actually inhabit them and force them to do their bidding. Some victims are made to jump in a lake, while others find themselves defending their captors against other attackers. Rarely do the "zombies" benefit from this strange behavior. Once their role in their predator's life cycle is over, they go from being "undead" to simply "dead."

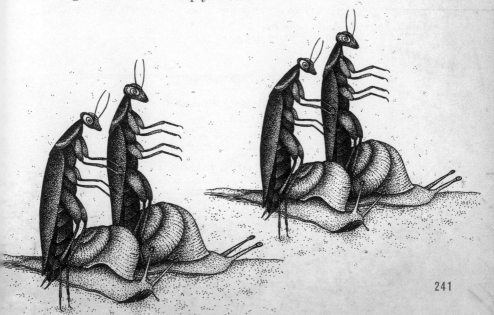

241

EMERALD COCKROACH WASP

Ampulex compressa

Also called a jewel wasp for its peacock green iridescent coloring, this diminutive wasp native to Asia and Africa is not afraid to tackle a much larger cockroach and force it to do its bidding. When the female is pregnant, she hunts down a cockroach and delivers a sting that briefly renders it immobile. That gives her a little time to work. She then slides her stinger directly into the roach's brain, delivering another sting that disables the roach's instinct to flee. Once she has gained control of it, she can lead it around by its antennae like a dog on a leash.

The roach follows the wasp into her nest and sits down obediently. She lays an egg on the roach's underside and leaves it in the nest, where it will wait patiently for the egg to hatch into a larva. The larva chews a hole in the roach's abdomen and crawls inside, spending the next week eating its internal organs and constructing a cocoon for itself. This eventually kills the roach, but the cocoon remains in its body for a month, then emerges from the cockroach as a full-grown adult, leaving nothing but the shell of the roach behind.

Once she has gained control
of the cockroach, the wasp can lead it
around by its antennae like
a dog on a leash.

TONGUE-EATING LOUSE
Cymothoa exigua

An aquatic crustacean resembling a pill bug, this creature enters the body of a fish through its gills and latches onto its tongue. It feeds upon the fish's tongue until there is nothing left but a stub. This doesn't bother the louse—it holds onto the stub, continuing to drink blood from it, and acts as a tongue so that the fish can continue to eat. From time to time, the parasites are found inside the mouths of whole snapper in fish markets, much to the horror of shoppers.

PARASITOID WASPS
Glyptapanteles sp

These wasps seek out specific species of caterpillars and lay up to eighty eggs inside them. There's nothing particularly unusual about that: many wasps lay eggs on or inside caterpillars. But these species do something different. Their eggs grow inside the body of the caterpillar, then hatch and leave to wrap themselves in cocoons on a nearby plant. The caterpillar survives this very invasive process and sticks around after the wasps move into the cocoon phase. If a predator, like a beetle or a stinkbug, approaches the cocoons, the caterpillar thrashes around and knocks the predator down. Once the wasps reach adulthood, they fly away and the caterpillar dies, having gained nothing from its strange protective behavior.

GREEN-BANDED BROODSAC
Leucochloridium paradoxum

In what is surely one of nature's most bizarre life cycles, this flatworm's eggs are secreted in bird droppings, where they must be eaten by snails in order to hatch. Once devoured, they move into the snail's digestive tract and emerge to form long tube structures that invade the snail's tentacles. At that point the snail cannot see or retract its tentacles. The tentacles, once invaded by this parasite, turn bright colors and wave around in the open, a behavior that is very attractive to birds. The birds swoop down and take a bite, which is exactly what the parasite wanted. Only when it is safely inside the body of a bird can it grow into adulthood and lay eggs, which are excreted in the bird's droppings so the cycle can begin again.

HAIRWORM
Spinochordodes tellinii

This parasitic worm begins its life as a microscopic larva, swimming around in water where it hopes to be swallowed by a grasshopper taking a drink. Once inside the grasshopper, it grows into adulthood, but it has a problem: it needs to get back into the water to find a mate. To accomplish this, it takes control of the grasshopper's brain—perhaps by releasing a protein that alters its central nervous system—and convinces its host to commit suicide by jumping into the nearest body of water. Once the grasshopper has drowned, the hairworm leaves the body and swims away.

PHORID FLY
Pseudacteon spp.

A tiny South American fly may be the solution to the fire ant problem in the American South. This fly injects its eggs into the fire ant. The larvae eat the ant's brains, causing the ant to wander aimlessly around for a week or two. Eventually the head falls off and the adult flies emerge in search of more fire ants to kill. This violent and vicious approach to pest control is deeply satisfying to people who have been plagued by the ants; researchers at the University of Texas are conducting experimental releases of the flies and assessing the implications of a wide-scale release.

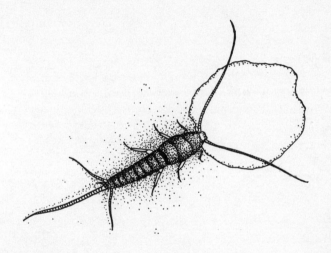

About the Artist

Briony Morrow-Cribbs creates copper etchings, fine bound books, and ceramic sculptures contained in "cabinets of curiosity" that reflect her fascination with the ways in which the rational language of science meets the mysterious and often grotesque world of nature.

A graduate of the Emily Carr Institute in Vancouver, British Columbia, and a master of fine arts candidate at the University of Wisconsin–Madison, Morrow-Cribbs's work has been shown in the United States and abroad.

She is the co-founder of Twin Vixen Press in Brattleboro, Vermont, and is represented by Davidson Galleries in Seattle and Brackenwood Gallery on Whidbey Island in Washington State.

Briony would like to thank Steven Krauth, the Distinguished Academic Curator of the Insect Research Collection at the University of Wisconsin–Madison, for his aid in the delicate work of insect research.

Resources

Visit WickedBugs.com for links to these
and other online resources.

INSECT IDENTIFICATION

Making an accurate identification of an insect or insect bite is best left to the experts. Carefully capturing the insect or taking a good photograph of it is critical to identifying it. Armed with this information, contact your county agricultural extension office or the entomology department at your local university for assistance.

The Entomological Society of America (www.entsoc.org) offers a resource section on its Web site with links to entomological societies and other insect-related information.

The American Arachnological Society (www.americanarachnology .org) offers a photo gallery, answers to commonly asked questions, and links to more resources.

The Royal Entomological Society (www.royensoc.co.uk) offers an online identification guide and other information about British bugs.

BugGuide.net is an online community of insect enthusiasts who post pictures of insects, spiders, and other creatures.

Buglife (www.buglife.org.uk) is a charity dedicated to the conservation of invertebrates, including Britain's rarest bugs.

INSECTARIUMS

Visiting an insectarium is a wonderful way to meet some of these creatures up close. Many natural history museums and zoos feature bug exhibits. Here are just a few of the more interesting insectariums around the world:

American Museum of Natural History, New York, NY (www .amnh.org). Holds one of the largest insect collections in the world; insect-related exhibits are a regular feature.

Audubon Insectarium, New Orleans, LA (www.auduboninstitute .org). The first major institution to open in New Orleans after Hurricane Katrina, this insect museum features live insect exhibits, a simulated underground encounter with human-sized bugs, and insect delicacies that brave children can sample in the cafeteria.

California Academy of Sciences, San Francisco, CA (www.calacademy.org). Features a four-story rain forest, natural history museum, educational naturalist center, and a living "green roof."

Field Museum, Chicago, IL (www.fieldmuseum.org). With an extraordinary insect and butterfly collection, this natural history museum regularly features special insect exhibits.

Montreal Insectarium, Montréal, Québec (www.ville.montreal .qc.ca/insectarium/). Live and preserved specimens, butterfly exhibits, and special programs.

Natural History Museum of Los Angeles County, Los Angeles, CA (www.nhm.org). Has an insect zoo with live specimens, along with regular "bug shows" where visitors can touch the creatures.

Natural History Museum, London, England (www.nhm.ac.uk). Known for its "creepy-crawly" exhibit, wildlife garden, and extraordinary Darwin Centre collection.

Smithsonian National Museum of Natural History, Washington, DC (www.mnh.si.edu). Includes an insect zoo, butterfly pavilion, and a vast collection of specimens.

PEST CONTROL

Correctly identifying pests is the first step to getting them out of your home and garden. Contact your county agricultural extension office or university entomology department for help identifying and controlling unwanted insects.

Almost every state has an integrated pest management (IPM) program to help eliminate pests using low-toxic approaches. Do a search online for your state's program; for instance, Illinois's program can be found at www.ipm.illinois.edu.

Pesticide Action Network North America (www.panna.org) offers a pesticide information database and information about alternatives to pesticides.

Pest Control UK (www.pestcontrol-uk.org) offers a selection of pest control resources for UK residents.

Richard Fagerlund (www.askthebugman.com) has been delivering sensible and safe pest control advice for years through his syndicated "Ask the Bugman" column and now through his Web site.

INSECT-TRANSMITTED DISEASES

The Centers for Disease Control (www.cdc.gov) and the National Health Service in the UK (www.nhs.uk) offer advice for travelers to minimize exposure to insect-transmitted disease and provide basic overviews of many of those diseases.

The World Health Organization (www.who.int) monitors and fights insect-transmitted disease outbreaks worldwide and offers basic health information for travelers.

The Carter Center (www.cartercenter.org) is working to eliminate a number of the diseases described in this book. Their strategies include teaching people how to build healthier latrines, distributing water filters, and offering free medication. Even a small donation can save a life; visit their Web site to find out more.

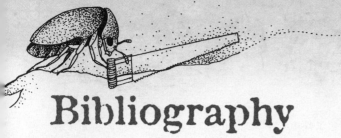

Bibliography

IDENTIFICATION GUIDES

Capinera, John L. *Encyclopedia of Entomology*. Dordrecht: Springer, 2008.

Eaton, Eric R., and Kenn Kaufman. *Kaufman Field Guide to Insects of North America*. New York: Houghton Mifflin, 2007.

Evans, Arthur V. *National Wildlife Federation Field Guide to Insects and Spiders and Related Species of North America*. New York: Sterling, 2007.

Foster, Steven, and Roger A. Caras. *A Field Guide to Venomous Animals and Poisonous Plants, North America, North of Mexico*. Peterson field guide series 46. Boston: Houghton Mifflin, 1994.

Haggard, Peter, and Judy Haggard. *Insects of the Pacific Northwest*. Timber Press field guide. Portland, OR: Timber Press, 2006.

Levi, Herbert Walter, Lorna Rose Levi, Herbert S. Zim, and Nicholas Strekalovsky. *Spiders and Their Kin*. New York: Golden Press, 1990.

O'Toole, Christopher. *Firefly Encyclopedia of Insects and Spiders*. Toronto: Firefly Books, 2002.

Resh, Vincent H., and Ring T. Cardé, eds. *Encyclopedia of Insects*. San Diego, CA: Elsevier Academic Press, 2009.

BIBLIOGRAPHY

MEDICAL REFERENCES

Goddard, Jerome. *Physician's Guide to Arthropods of Medical Importance*. Boca Raton, FL: CRC Press, 2007.

Lane, Richard P., and Roger Ward Crosskey. *Medical Insects and Arachnids*. London: Chapman & Hall, 1993.

Mullen, Gary R., and Lance A. Durden. *Medical and Veterinary Entomology*. Amsterdam: Academic Press, 2002.

PEST CONTROL

Ellis, Barbara W., Fern Marshall Bradley, and Helen Atthowe. *The Organic Gardener's Handbook of Natural Insect and Disease Control: A Complete Problem-Solving Guide to Keeping Your Garden and Yard Healthy without Chemicals*. Emmaus, PA: Rodale Press, 1996.

Gillman, Jeff. *The Truth About Garden Remedies: What Works, What Doesn't, and Why*. Portland, OR: Timber Press, 2008.

Gillman, Jeff. *The Truth About Organic Gardening: Benefits, Drawbacks, and the Bottom Line*. Portland, OR: Timber Press, 2008.

FURTHER READING

Alexander, John O'Donel. *Arthropods and Human Skin*. Berlin: Springer-Verlag, 1984.

Berenbaum, May R. *Bugs in the System: Insects and Their Impact on Human Affairs*. Reading, MA: Addison-Wesley, 1995.

Bondeson, Jan. *A Cabinet of Medical Curiosities*. Ithaca, NY: Cornell University Press, 1997.

Burgess, Jeremy, Michael Marten, and Rosemary Taylor. *Microcosmos*. Cambridge: Cambridge University Press, 1987.

Byrd, Jason H., and James L. Castner. *Forensic Entomology: The Utility of Arthropods in Legal Investigations*. Boca Raton, FL: CRC Press, 2001.

Campbell, Christopher. *The Botanist and the Vintner: How Wine Was Saved for the World*. Chapel Hill, NC: Algonquin Books of Chapel Hill, 2005.

Carwardine, Mark. *Extreme Nature*. New York: Collins, 2005.

Chase, Marilyn. *The Barbary Plague: The Black Death in Victorian San Francisco*. New York: Random House, 2003.

Chinery, Michael. *Amazing Insects: Images of Fascinating Creatures*. Buffalo, NY: Firefly Books, 2008.

Cloudsley-Thompson, J. L. *Insects and History*. New York: St. Martin's Press, 1976.

Collinge, Sharon K., and Chris Ray. *Disease Ecology: Community Structure and Pathogen Dynamics*. Oxford: Oxford University Press, 2006.

Cowan, Frank. *Curious Facts in the History of Insects; Including Spiders and Scorpions: A Complete Collection of the Legends, Superstitions, Beliefs, and Ominous Signs Connected with Insects, Together with Their Uses in Medicine, Art, and as Food; and a Summary of Their Remarkable Injuries and Appearances*. Philadelphia: J. B. Lippincott, 1865.

Crosby, Molly Caldwell. *The American Plague: The Untold Story of Yellow Fever, the Epidemic That Shaped Our History*. New York: Berkley Books, 2006.

Crosskey, Roger Ward. *The Natural History of Blackflies*. Chichester, England: Wiley, 1990.

Eisner, Thomas. *For Love of Insects*. Cambridge, MA: Belknap Press of Harvard University Press, 2003.

Eisner, Thomas, Maria Eisner, and Melody Siegler. *Secret Weapons: Defenses of Insects, Spiders, Scorpions, and Other Many-Legged*

Creatures. Cambridge, MA: Belknap Press of Harvard University Press, 2005.

Erzinclioglu, Zakaria. *Maggots, Murder, and Men: Memories and Reflections of a Forensic Entomologist*. New York: Thomas Dunne Books, 2000.

Evans, Arthur V. *What's Bugging You? A Fond Look at the Animals We Love to Hate*. Charlottesville: University of Virginia Press, 2008.

Evans, Howard Ensign. *Life on a Little-Known Planet*. New York: Dutton, 1968.

Friedman, Reuben. *The Emperor's Itch: The Legend Concerning Napoleon's Affliction with Scabies*. New York: Froben Press, 1940.

Gennard, Dorothy E. *Forensic Entomology: An Introduction*. Chichester, England: Wiley, 2007.

Glausiusz, Josie, and Volker Steger. *Buzz: The Intimate Bond between Humans and Insects*. San Francisco: Chronicle Books, 2004.

Goff, M. Lee. *A Fly for the Prosecution: How Insect Evidence Helps Solve Crimes*. Cambridge, MA: Harvard University Press, 2000.

Gordon, Richard. *An Alarming History of Famous and Difficult! Patients: Amusing Medical Anecdotes from Typhoid Mary to FDR*. New York: St. Martin's Press, 1997.

Gratz, Norman. *The Vector- and Rodent-Borne Diseases of Europe and North America: Their Distribution and Public Health Burden*. Cambridge: Cambridge University Press, 2006.

Gullan, P. J., and P. S. Cranston. *The Insects: An Outline of Entomology*. Malden, MA: Blackwell, 2005.

Hickin, Norman E. *Bookworms: The Insect Pests of Books*. London: Sheppard Press, 1985.

Hoeppli, Reinhard. *Parasitic Diseases in Africa and the Western*

Hemisphere: Early Documentation and Transmission by the Slave Trade. Basel: Verlag fur Recht und Gesellschaft, 1969.

Holldobler, Bert, and Edward O. Wilson. *The Ants.* Cambridge, MA: Belknap Press of Harvard University Press, 1990.

Holldobler, Bert, and Edward O. Wilson. *The Superorganism: The Beauty, Elegance, and Strangeness of Insect Societies.* New York: W.W. Norton, 2009.

Howell, Michael, and Peter Ford. *The Beetle of Aphrodite and Other Medical Mysteries.* New York: Random House, 1985.

Hoyt, Erich, and Ted Schultz. *Insect Lives: Stories of Mystery and Romance from a Hidden World.* Cambridge, MA: Harvard University Press, 2002.

Jones, David E. *Poison Arrows: North American Indian Hunting and Warfare.* Austin: University of Texas Press, 2007.

Kelly, John. *The Great Mortality: An Intimate History of the Black Death, the Most Devastating Plague of All Time.* New York: HarperCollins, 2005.

Lockwood, Jeffrey Alan. *Locust: The Devastating Rise and Mysterious Disappearance of the Insect That Shaped the American Frontier.* New York: Basic Books, 2004.

Lockwood, Jeffrey Alan. *Six-Legged Soldiers: Using Insects as Weapons of War.* Oxford: Oxford University Press, 2009.

Marks, Isaac Meyer. *Fears and Phobias.* Personality and psychopathology 5. New York: Academic Press, 1969.

Marley, Christopher. *Pheromone: The Insect Artwork of Christopher Marley.* San Francisco: Pomegranate, 2008.

Mayor, Adrienne. *Greek Fire, Poison Arrows, and Scorpion Bombs: Biological and Chemical Warfare in the Ancient World.* Woodstock, NY: Overlook Duckworth, 2003.

Mertz, Leslie A. *Extreme Bugs*. New York: Collins, 2007.

Mingo, Jack, Erin Barrett, and Lucy Autrey Wilson. *Cause of Death: A Perfect Little Guide to What Kills Us*. New York: Pocket Books, 2008.

Murray, Polly. *The Widening Circle: A Lyme Disease Pioneer Tells Her Story*. New York: St. Martin's Press, 1996.

Myers, Kathleen Ann, and Nina M. Scott. *Fernandez de Oviedo's Chronicle of America: A New History for a New World*. Austin: University of Texas Press, 2008.

Nagami, Pamela. *Bitten: True Medical Stories of Bites and Stings*. New York: St. Martin's Press, 2004.

Naskrecki, Piotr. *The Smaller Majority: The Hidden World of the Animals That Dominate the Tropics*. Cambridge, MA: Belknap Press of Harvard University Press, 2005.

Neuwinger, Hans Dieter. *African Ethnobotany: Poisons and Drugs: Chemistry, Pharmacology, Toxicology*. London: Chapman & Hall, 1996.

O'Toole, Christopher. *Alien Empire: An Exploration of the Lives of Insects*. New York: HarperCollins, 1995.

Preston-Mafham, Ken, and Rod Preston-Mafham. *The Natural World of Bugs and Insects*. San Diego, CA: Thunder Bay, 2001.

Resh, Vincent H., and Ring T. Carde. *Encyclopedia of Insects*. Amsterdam: Academic Press, 2003.

Riley, Charles V. *The Locust Plague in the United States: Being More Particularly a Treatise on the Rocky Mountain Locust or So-Called Grasshopper, as It Occurs East of the Rocky Mountains, with Practical Recommendations for Its Destruction*. Chicago: Rand, McNally, 1877.

Rosen, William. *Justinian's Flea: The First Great Plague, and the End of the Roman Empire*. New York: Penguin Books, 2008.

Rule, Ann. *Empty Promises and Other True Cases*. New York: Pocket Books, 2001.

Schaeffer, Neil. *The Marquis de Sade: A Life*. New York: Knopf, 1999.

Talty, Stephan. *The Illustrious Dead: The Terrifying Story of How Typhus Killed Napoleon's Greatest Army*. New York: Crown, 2009.

Ventura, Varla. *The Book of the Bizarre: Freaky Facts and Strange Stories*. York Beach, ME: Red Wheel/Weiser, 2008.

Wade, Nicholas. *The New York Times Book of Insects*. Guilford, CT: Lyons Press, 2003.

Waldbauer, Gilbert. *Insights from Insects: What Bad Bugs Can Teach Us*. Amherst, NY: Prometheus Books, 2005.

Walters, Martin. *The Illustrated World Encyclopedia of Insects: A Natural History and Identification Guide to Beetles, Flies, Bees, Wasps, Mayflies, Dragonflies, Cockroaches, Mantids, Earwigs, Ants and Many More*. London: Lorenz, 2008.

Weiss, Harry B., and Ralph Herbert Carruthers. *Insect Enemies of Books*. New York: The New York Public Library, 1937.

Williams, Greer. *The Plague Killers*. New York: Charles Scribner's Sons, 1969.

Zinsser, Hans. *Rats, Lice, and History*. London: Penguin, 2000.

Index